REQUIRES ASSEMBLY

NEWSPAPER DESIGN AND PRODUCTION
BY MIKE BARKER

THE STUDENT PRESS
www.thestudentpress.org

AN IMPRINT OF
MIKE BARKER DESIGN

Copyright © Mike Barker, 2006

All rights reserved. No part of this publication may be reproduced in any form without prior written consent of the publisher. Any requests for photocopying of any part of this book should be directed in writing to the Canadian Copyright Licensing Agency.

PRINTED IN CANADA

Second Edition
9 8 7 6 5 4 3 2 1

Barker, Mike, 1976–
    Requires Assembly: Newspaper design and
    production / Mike Barker

Includes bibliographic references.

ISBN: 0-9780807-0-X

The Student Press
An imprint of Mike Barker Design
Suite 1909 – 10 Hogarth Avenue
Toronto, Ontario M4K 1J9

www.thestudentpress.org

The Student Press, for the life long student

ⓘ INTRODUCTION

Welcome	vi
About this book	vii
To the Editor	viii
To the Designer	ix

STEP ONE
BASICS

1.0	Introduction	11
1.1	Basics of Design	12
1.2	Basics of News Design	17
1.3	Terms	28

STEP TWO
DESIGN

2.0	Introduction	33
2.1	Before designing a news page	34
2.2	Type basics	37
2.3	Text elements	46
2.4	Design elements	54
2.5	The whole page	58
2.6	Template and style guide	64
2.7	Colour	70
2.8	The next step	74

STEP THREE
PRODUCTION

3.0	introduction	81
3.1	pre-press	92
3.2	production management	100
3.3	pdf 101	105

OTHER

Index	108
Colophon	111
About the author	112
Acknowledgements	112

Welcome

Welcome to Requires Assembly: Newspaper design and production. Producing a newspaper requires some labour, though not as physical as it once was, but some work is involved in pulling the pieces together. Getting from edited news to the printed paper requires assembly.

A newspaper is made of a collection of elements (parts) and these need to be assembled in a logical way. In many ways this is the instruction manual you get with the living room furniture you bought in one easy to carry box. And the computer is your allen key—the tool to secure the parts together.

Design is fundmental to your newspaper, but the news must always remain the most important element in the newspaper. This information ranges from hard hitting news, profiles, arts coverage to lengthy features. Design has an important role in telling the news—both in the design of the newspaper and the way information is conveyed.

Not too long ago, newspapers were produced without a computer. Design consisted of the layout of news stories and other graphic elements—the structure to the page used to complement the news and attract the reader. This was done by hand mostly, in production where these elements were pasted to a large sheet of paper with a grid of light blue lines. These "flats" were delivered the printer to be photographed, the negatives used to burn plates which were strapped to the press.

Today production and design are done together, mostly on a computer. Yet there are similarities to the past. A structure is still designed that is both attractive to the eye and serves the content. And the actual act of laying out the pages is done on the pasteboard on the computer, often by the copy editor.

Recently I spoke to an editor from the first student newspaper I worked at. The design has changed over the years, but some elements have stayed the same, including the body text typeface. As my first major redesign I can honestly say that I am amazed elements still remain, but then again, wise choices were made back then. During my most recent redesign, the paper chose to shrink the page length to a smaller tabloid which was easier for reading on transit. But this time, as I rushed a redesign through in one weekend, I understood where the mistakes can be made and how to do the issue properly. Both times, the redesign was done to between issues, yet both times, there were a few editions to work out the bugs. A paper's design is not always static, rather it can be a living and flexible system.

About This Book

Requires Assembly began as a resource primarily for student newspapers and has evolved into a resource essential for any newspaper. Even an editor, writer, advertising buyer, graphic designer, student or teacher will find this resource helpful. Throughout this book the references to a student newspaper and the campus community can be applied directly to any newspaper large and small regardless of the community it serves.

While design and production go hand in hand, there are some distinct reasons to separate the two aspects. Design follows a lot of the theory and thinking behind how the news is told visually. The design is the underlying structure or foundation on which the news is supported. Production is the technical side of producing a newspaper. Just as the computer aids in designing the visual identity or graphic style of your newspaper, the computer also assembles the news stories and pages, then creates the PDF or produces the printouts for your printer.

This book has been divided into three steps. Starting from the beginning, Basics, highlights the foundational information helpful to understanding the language in the remaining sections, and covers the theory and terminlogy of design and newspaper production. Design, specifically focuses on the elements that go into each page's design and how these elements are used. This section focuses on how the news can be told visually through an understanding of page composition. Finally, Production, is geared especially to understanding the technical side of producing the publication.

While the information has been structured for easy reference, each part is relevant toward building the final product. Throughout the book, a fictional newspaper—designed with real news copy—is used to present the examples discussed.

To The Editor

These few words are to comfort you. Design is important to your newspaper, but it does not supersede news. The news is the most important element of a newspaper. Design can support the news in two ways.

First, design supports the news by communicating the information in the most unblemished way. Good idea in this way is the structure—the framing and foundation of a house—yet it is invisable. Readers do notice bad design, even if they are unable to verbalise why the news is hard to read.

Second, design can be used to tell a story or relate the news in a different way. Your designer should be included in story meetings. The newspaper designer is a journalist who uses structure, typography and visual storytelling. Often there is news too boring to run in words—budget details for example. Stats make for boring news, but often a few gems exist which can be told through information graphics. This is especially true for information that might otherwise be in a sidebar. A visual sidebar on the five biggest expeditures at your school might make for an eye-catching image that will be invite readers into an indepth article on waste.

News design does not have to be approached by a designer who sees themself as an artist. An editor might also layout news, viewing themself as a section editor, editing the page. On the otherhand, a technical person with neither strong a fine art or journalism knowledge will see a newspaper in technical terms, as a structured and ordered page.

All of these people can do justice to the newspaper.

Honour your designer with the best content possible. A designer needs something to be proud of and being given poor copy serves no one—not the designer, you or the reader.

To The Designer

Ask yourself, why you are designing for this newspaper? You take words and fience them into well designed news, readable to the viewer. You are also a storyteller, at the paper just like a journalist, able to observe and relate to the reader the essential information. Design is important to the newspaper. It lends structure and order, why also being visually appealling. But the content is the most important element. Your editor's job is to provide the best content. Your job is to honour that content. David Carson may be a great designer, but using dingbats or unreadable type does not serve the reader. Of course there is a time and place of that, do not worry.

Your role as a designer is to be included in the story meetings and news gathering. You are a journalist, even if you are unable to ask the questions and form the words as magically as your paper's writers. Instead as a visual person, you will see the news an entirely different way and being able to rel-ate that to the reader improves your paper. For example, your editor assigns a writer to your city or town council meeting. You should go too and see how you could cover the same meeting—possibly by sketching the scene similar to a court drawing. The illustration can add colour to a story some readers might not find interesting—and since few students will see the inside of the senate chambers, a parallel can be created to a court drawing which captures a scene a camera is not allowed to.

Design is used in two ways to serve the news: to communicate the essential information in an article by creating perfectly typeset copy that is readable; and in telling the news visually. Your job may not be to write or edit the news, but you have to tell the story. That's equally as important. Good luck. ∎

STEP ONE
BASICS

1.0   Introduction

Step one begins very simply: with the basics. This step focuses on the Basics of Design, the Basics of News Design, and providing some terminology on both news design and production. The first part of this section will explore the Principles of Design, which are just eight loose rules that have been observed in design. Like the Principles of Design, the approach to the Basics of News Design is in theory. This step is meant to get you thinking about how to analyze design, how to question the importance of news, how to serve the information contained in the news, and how to serve the reader. Every publication should have an idea of its readership. By understanding their readers habits publications can deliver the best paper possible. News design begins with an understanding of why a newspaper should be designed and the basic elements with which the designer and editor should be familiar. The designer and the editor should find this guide helpful in understanding how design plays a pivotal role in telling the news.

1.1 Basics of Design

Design does not have a set of hard and fast rules that can be applied. The perfect formula has yet to be discovered. Good design is perceived, partly as a matter of personal taste, but also because the design adheres to good composition rules. There are a few principles to guide the composition, called the design principles. These principles differ from author to author and some principles here might not be included by another author's own list.

1.1.1 CONTRAST

Two or more objects looking strikingly different from one another—in sharp juxtaposition or closely related. There are several ways to contrast visual elements: size or scale, shape or volume, position (relationship to other objects), direction, color and tone or value. Size is one of the easiest ways to achieve contrast between two or more objects—the larger headline will catch the reader's eye first. Contrast stands as its own principle, but can be found in other principles, such as emphasis and positive/negative space.

Contrast: one square stands out because the shape's colour contrasts against the background.

1.1.2 EMPHASIS

Emphasis can be placed on an element a number of ways, but most basically through shape, such as white space, size or cropping. Contrast, dominance and isolation draw emphasis to an object. A green ball on a lawn doesn't stand out as well as a white ball. An exercise ball would dominate over a field of tennis balls from its sheer size. And isolating one tennis ball from a large pile draws the eye to the one ball.

An object should stand out and be the focal point for the reader. The focal point is the place on the page the designer wants the reader's eyes to gravitate toward first. In news design this is key to structuring a hierarchy on the page, from the more dominant news article to the least.

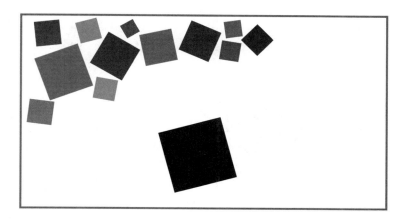

Emphasis: the large black square has been isolated from the remaining shapes and set in a contrasting shade.

1.1.3 BALANCE

There are two specific forms of balance in graphic design: symmetrical—equal weight mirrors on either side of an axis creating a uniform and proportionate style; and asymmetrical—not being equally balanced and looking disproportionate. An asymmetrical page will be more lively and dynamic, while a symmetrical page will be static and clean. Perfect balance has its place, especially when aiming for a calming page.

Balance: symmetrical (left) and asymmetrical (right) balance.

1.1.4 POSITIVE/NEGATIVE SPACE

Also called the figure and the ground, the negative space contrasts with the positive space. We are very much used to white paper (negative) with black type (the positive), but on black paper, white text is the positive. Negative space forms the shape of the positive figure; without the striking contrast, type would be hard to read. Balancing the two spaces creates simple and very effective design—logos such as the World Wildlife Foundation's panda are simple solid shapes with negative space forming half of the picture.

Positive/negative: this logo uses negative space (the white) to crave the lines into the black shape.

1.1.5 MOVEMENT/DIRECTION

An image can contain movement, which will guide the reader in a particular direction. Photographs illustrating a moving car or person obviously invite the reader to follow their path. Even a still model with eyes looking left creates a direction. Both these principles can be applied to forming an eye flow created by the movement or direction of not only the imagery, but also the text elements.

Movement/direction: this image has a downward angled direction and the shapes appear to be moving in that direction.

1.1.6 REPETITION

When any individual element is used more than once, repetition occurs. Repeating an object creates a rhythm and varying the distance between objects will change that rhythm. Consider that the objects represent a beat, which can remain even, then change like a musical chord. Repetition has the potential to create visual continuity, though it can become monotonous, just as repetition in one's activities can be boring. Adding a variation or deviation to the regular pattern can create a stimulating visual break. In summary, contrasting elements can break the rhythm of a group of repetitive elements.

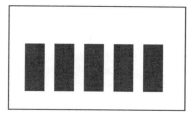

Repetition: the shapes on the left are evenly spaced and equal in size, creating a rhythm. To the right, the rhythm is altered with the angled shape.

1.1.7 FRAME OF REFERENCE

The edge of a page forms the frame of reference for most newspaper readers. Most newspapers print in a margin surrounding the outside edge on a page, making all design self-contained within this border. For photos on the page, a rule, or straight line, drawn around the image forms the boundary for the reader, especially in photos with negative space that matches the paper (often the sky). Another way to contain the image is through cropping, which changes the frame of reference for the reader — the cropped imagery is not available to the reader and can focus a photo to one person in a group.

1.1.8 UNITY / GESTALT

It is human nature to seek patterns in our visual world. Gestalt theory recognizes that the parts of a visual image may be individually examined or considered, but the whole of the image is greater and different from the sum of the parts. Realizing that patterns can be formed can increase the effectiveness of communication—creating a pattern will make it easy for the viewer to search for one. Below is an example of separate dots that can be seen individually, but together the pattern is understood as an arrow, which is a greater concept than the given parts. Through proximity, emphasis is explained because of gestalt—two squares inside a frame of reference placed far from each other create a pattern and the mind attempts to understand their relationship to each other. Completion or closure is another principle of gestalt. The viewer closes several separate curved lines into a circle filling the gaps left out.

When all the elements in a design are combined properly, there is a complete unity. Do all the elements add up to make the overall composition? If not, what is missing or what elements are not necessary for the composition?

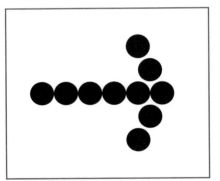 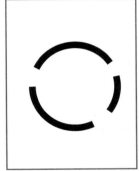

Gestalt: a collection of dots grouped in a pattern create an arrow(left) — the sum of these parts make a greater image. The eye closes the separate curved lines into a circle.

1.2 Basics of News Design

The basic structure of news design has been around for over a century. There are also plenty of basic ideas and beliefs that pertain to why newspapers look as they do today. When it comes to the design of newspapers a balancing act must be achieved between designing a newspaper's look to separate it from others and the restrictions current printing technology allows. Today it has never been easier to design and layout a newspaper. Twenty years from now, it will be even easier.

Technology has allowed papers to go to press faster and print more color on more pages. The remaining hurdle is still the time it takes to distribute newspapers affordably. Presses are becoming more efficient, but not substantially faster, and the page size is changing as the press shrinks. Printing 5,000 copies of a 16-page tabloid newspaper takes less than 30 minutes—more time is spent setting up the press and fine-tuning the registration. Pre-press times have lessened as papers upload their pages directly to the printer's server and skip the extra trip with the camera-ready flats. Still, someone has to go to the printer and bring back all those bundles of papers.

There are many constants and plenty of variables. A good newspaper design is meant to create a consistent look that is flexible enough to vary with the day-to-day change in the news. With advances in technology occurring more often, papers need to redesign to adjust to the change—often this is because of improvements that then show deficiencies that may have been intentional previously. As the presses improve, type and photography reproduction improves and the custom typeface meant to fix the shortcomings of the previous press will look bad on the new one. Readers constantly want news, but the way it's delivered and the speed changes. Thanks to the Internet, readers expect their news immediately, which allows papers to meet that expectation on the Internet and use the traditional paper to further expand the news beyond the simple facts immediately after an event.

In his book *Functional News Design*, Edmund C. Arnold offered four purposes for newspapers to be laid out—at a time when the news page wasn't thought out: 1. To increase readability and to attract the reader into the news; 2. To sort the news so the reader knows at a glance which are the most important stories; 3. To create attractive and interesting pages; 4. To create recognition, to make the reader identify and want your paper as soon as he sees it.

Arnold's four principles still hold true today and are described in his book in great detail. The principles do not apply design rules to the process of news design. Today, the principles would combine the understanding and value of design and be worded slightly differently:
1. Sustain readability and create multiple visual and information entry points into the news.
2. Build a visual hierarchy on each page to lead the reader's eye in order of importance.
3. Design pages that visually explain the news in creative and engaging ways.
4. Create a visual identity for your paper that defines and differentiates your product.

1.2.1 THE ELEMENTS OF NEWSPAPER DESIGN

Newspaper design is often referred to as a "kit of parts" or a jigsaw puzzle. Calling it a jigsaw puzzle would suggest only one design can be achieved, but there are many ways of approaching the design of a page. Wooden blocks make a good metaphor because there are countless ways in which the blocks can be assembled.

Take those blocks and restrict their movement into a frame. The pieces now compose a puzzle where the varying shaped blocks represent different elements on the newspaper page. Thinking of the page in this way requires visualizing the elements as separate parts that can be jumbled in various configurations. Each issue, those same wooden blocks are assembled in different ways, but are essentially the same blocks: nameplate, folio or header, headline, body text, photos and graphics, photo captions, pullquotes and rules.

Early news layout was very much a timely process for shuffling page elements around to fit. The full evolution will be explained further on; however, the basic developments were in five methods: movable type, hot metal typesetting, photo typesetting, paste up

and computer aided. The first four represent two pairs: physical lead type to camera-ready artwork. Movable lead type gave way to lead type cast in full lines, paragraphs or even whole pages. The early movable type and line-casting machines created movable lead blocks that were assembled much like the wooden block metaphor. Even paste up started with photo typesetting and evolved with the computer and laser printer. The same four methods were pre-digital physical production processes that required moving type and other physical elements around the page. Now the method of production is digital with some papers still using paste up via laser printer, camera-ready art, which is not yet entirely digital.

Even still, the process is done in the digital world on a computer. The two-dimensional world has become disconnected from the three-dimensional process of building a page, but the steps are similar.

1.2.2 BEGIN WITH THE READER

While the news is the most important element of the newspaper, there must be an audience. Student newspapers for example are community papers, the community being the school it serves. Consider the community the paper serves; the staff at a paper reflects members of the community, and they likely understand what local readers want to read.

A commuter campus would be well served by a small, easy-to-hold newspaper that can be read on transit. A predominately residence-based campus can have a larger paper and may want to cover the nightlife on and off campus.

HOLDING THE READER:

Newspapers don't have captive audiences that will read the paper from cover to cover. Numerous studies have shown the amount of time an average person spends reading a given publication. One research survey specifically looked at the reading habits of Canadian students and found that, on average, students spend 21 minutes reading their student paper (CCMR). Remember, as a student journalist, you likely read more than the average amount. Your reader doesn't.

Read through your current issue for 21 minutes and see how far you get. Unless you are a speed-reader or the paper only has three pages of news, you probably didn't finish the entire paper. Your readers are likely to head for their favorite section, be that news, arts or sports. Once the reader is in one section and reading an article, far less than half will finish reading the rest of the page.

Does your paper want to move readers through the entire paper quickly or let them pick off the best parts? This is where design and good copy writing can help. The way newspapers serve the reader's needs has to adapt to changes in technology. Even without a website, student papers are still the best source for news on their campuses. And there is a simple choice in how all information is covered—reach as many readers as possible with a paper that serves to inform readers even if they only casually flip through the paper. Not all readers want long news stories and most will want to be able to pick and choose what to read easily, so make it easy for the reader to get there quickly.

1.2.3 COLUMN WIDTH AND THE READING SPEED

A reader's speed is controlled by a number of factors in the design: type size, legibility and column size. Narrow columns help the reader move quickly through the article, which may be good for news, but not optimal for a feature. A few longer columns contrasted with shorter ones will also control reading speed. A further explanation of finding the correct column width is related to the design and typeface choice, expanded in the Design section.

1.2.4 INFORMATION IS THE NEWS

Lengthy articles have an important place in the paper. Indeed, deep analysis is what newspapers are able to do with all the space provided within. Since the average student reader will spend 21 minutes reading the paper—less than the 44 minutes or more of a television newscast—a balance needs to be made between all the news and the most important information.

Most newspapers use the headline plus a sub-headline or deck to entice the reader in. It acts as a teaser meant to give a hint, but not the full story. Some free daily papers cut the news down to a minimal amount, creating a long news bite. A trend is also emerging where papers take the essential information of a story and write a short story of 100–200 words. Done properly and combined with the full story, this can inform readers and tease them into an article.

Sum up a story in less than 50 words and use this as a "window" or pull-quote to place near the article. While this may seem like the Cliff Notes of news writing, it can allow the "nutgraph" to explain the entire article outside the story's copy. Striking a balance can deliver the news and still allow students to get a broad sense of the entire paper.

1.2.5 THE FORMAT

Newspapers have traditionally been divided into two formats: the broadsheet and the tabloid. Along with these physical shapes is the cultural importance we place on those formats. In North America, like in parts of Europe, the broadsheet is the serious and respected business and ruling elite newspaper; the tabloid

Format: current newspapers range in size but usually conform to one of three formats—broadsheet (approx. 13.5" x 23"), tabloid (approx. 11.5" x 14") and Berliner (approx. 12.25" x 18").

is a worker's paper with crass headlines that define "if it bleeds, it leads". Those lines are slowly blurring, although this is happening slower in North American than in Europe. In Spain, tabloids deliver serious news and in Germany broadsheets vary in content between that of a traditional broadsheet (Frankfurter Allgemeine) and one with tabloid content (Bild). A new format is in the game, a hybrid that combines the importance of the broadsheet in a smaller and thus easier to read format—the Berliner.

The Society for News Design chose for their 27th edition of best newspaper designs in the world, a redesigned Guardian. As one of two chosen, The Guardian not only changed their graphic style but also morphed from a broadsheet to Berliner. The Berliner—modeled after the newspaper, Berliner Zeitung—is smaller than a broadsheet yet still folded in the middle. Because of changes in press sizes, more papers may move to the Berliner format out of necessity. The smaller format is easier to handle and is the perfect hybrid between the two sizes. However, advertising sales are mostly based on the ad size—a full-page broadsheet ad is bigger and more expensive than one in a tabloid. Consequently, broadsheets haven't switched to the new size because advertising rates would be reduced and papers would be making less.

Student newspapers in Canada have the unique advantage of being almost entirely tabloids with at least two exceptions. Few of those papers have reason to move to either a broadsheet or Berliner format. Instead they use the tabloid format for serious news—basically producing the weekly magazine-style newspaper that alternative weeklies copied.

1.2.6 VISUAL IDENTITY

A company's brand is its' visual identity—which is more than just a logo. Many corporations have ether custom-designed typefaces or a set typeface used in all advertising, product literature and internal documents. Along with the logo—or system of logos for larger multi-division companies—and the typeface, a corporation will have a style for how each item is designed to keep consistency. A corporation wants to appear as one entity across all products. Time Magazine may have several editions around the world and websites for each, but the cover of every issue has the same Time logo and red border. Readers can then identify a copy of Time very easily.

Consider how the mind works in recognizing almost anything in our environment—first through shape, then color and finally content. The distinct shape of the Apple logo immediately conjures the fruit—the shape is a pictograph for an apple. Then one's eye will recognize the color, either the rainbow or solid color, and then the content or context of the logo. In this case it is the pictograph that means Apple, the company, not the crunchy fruit. With that association comes computers and iPods.

When it comes to newspapers, each has a distinct visual style that separates it from other newspapers and reinforces its own consistent brand. Apart from looking different on the newsstand, each page should have a visual relationship with all others and still allow for flexibility to define each section of a paper. Just as a corporation's visual identity is more than a logo, the identity of a newspaper goes beyond the nameplate—the paper's logo—to the choice of typefaces, graphic elements and page construction.

A distinct visual identity is important for a paper, especially in a competitive market where the publication has to stand out. The problem: all newspapers basically look the same. One informed study by a design firm removed the nameplates from six daily papers in the United States, leaving six very similar papers. When the National Post was launched it had to look very different from the other Toronto and national papers, including the Globe and Mail and even others across Canada. Of all the current broadsheet daily papers in Canada, Montreal's La Presse is the most distinct. Take a look at your local papers and compare the covers with the nameplate removed—do this among the papers that match your format.

The first Canadian daily to switch to a Berliner will have a great advantage in being distinct.

While there needs to be consistency, that doesn't mean each page and section must look exactly the same. Within one page, the identity of each section needs to be different and recognizable. Consider again how the reader will view the paper—first impression will be through the shape. Not just the physical shape of the paper, but the shapes on the page. If the sports section uses a different skybox structure for its front page than other sections, readers will look for that element as much as the title.

When approaching the redesign of a newspaper, its previous style and brand should be considered, as well as distinguishing the paper from the competition.

1.2.7 HISTORY OF NEWS LAYOUT

The computer you use to lay out the newspaper deserves a big hug. The current popular method of preparing the pages for the printer has improved over the last 100 years. Creating a PDF and sending it to the printer has replaced one method only recently—paste up.

Even when computers joined newspapers, pages were printed by laser printer and "pasted up" using hot wax. These camera-ready pages were taken to the printer on large flats, and then photographed. This created a large negative that was then transferred on to the printing press. The PDF takes out that step while removing the possibility of affecting the paper's quality when relying on an old laser printer and a half-full toner cartridge.

Johann Gutenberg is credited with the invention of printing. Gutenberg more appropriately took established technologies and improved them. The Chinese had perfected relief printing and around 1040 C.E. Pi Sheng discovered moveable type. Paper had arrived some nine centuries before in 105 C.E. Gutenberg took relief-printing theory, the concept of moveable type and the availability of paper and perfected it in the form of his famous press and lead type casting.

Mass printing was born and presses spread across Europe during the Renaissance, quickly finding artisans ready to explore the new craft. When Gutenberg built his press, he wanted to print the Bible, set in a type very close to the calligraphic masters of the era. In the several hundred years that followed, type evolved from the wide pen stroked black letter to the modern roman and italics typefaces. The printing press became a tool for spreading ideas throughout Europe and the North American colonies. Design historians point to the oldest surviving newspaper, the Avisa Relation oder Zeitung, which began printing in Germany on a regular basis in 1609.

The modern concept of a newspaper was far away, but the human desire to spread news and ideas was aided by the press—to print broadsides, pamphlets, tracts and eventually newspapers. The Gutenberg press started a revolution, but for over 3 centuries, printing spread slowly. When the Industrial Revolution was bringing the powered machine to the factory, printing finally saw innovation first with a cast iron press in 1800, and then with the first steam-powered press in 1804.

Just as in Gutenberg's era, three elements had to come together for printing to evolve. First the powered presses that went from 250 small sheets per hour in 1800 to 4,000 double-sided, 35" x 22" sheets in 1827. The Times of London was printing more copies, faster, sooner andcheaper. The Fourdrinier machine brought the Industrial Revolution to paper and the ability to create large rolls of paper was achieved. By the mid-1800s, it was possible to print 25,000 copies an hour, yet the composing room was filled with typesetters who labored away, hand-setting each letter in every word in every newspaper—a slow and costly process. Finally, in 1886 Ottmar Mergenthaler demonstrated the fruits of his ten years of struggle—his keyboard-operated linecasting machine. It set entire lines of type at once, and the Linotype machine was born.

Handmade paper, hand set type and the hand press were all now replaced by machines that were faster and more accurate. This evolution allowed newspapers to become more frequent with bigger editions. Through the 1900s, news production evolved slowly until offset web presses replaced the lead cast presses, which were still in operation in the 1970s.

Newspapers were rarely daily until linecasting machines were invented and revolutionized news production from single letter by single letter typesetting to an automated approach. The linecaster released each letter with the push of a button while the previous method required each letter to be chosen from a drawer and placed in a composer's stick the right way up. These tiny letters required good eyesight. But both methods of news production relied on filling the page, with news edited to fit the space available.

Each page was not planned out as carefully as one done today and multiple column headlines didn't appear until after 1900. Articles were usually written as one column of text due to the ease of moving around just one column if late breaking news proved of greater importance. Newspapers were designed vertically and only in the 1980s did the horizontal look become more widely used.

1.2.8 THE FUTURE OF NEWS LAYOUT

Newspapers are slowly changing around the world. It's an evolution that may someday see most newspapers in tabloid format. There are sociological changes: the Internet and the growth in free dailies are affecting society. Readers care less about the relationship between the format and the approach to news coverage. But even as readers become increasingly more comfortable with the tabloid format, the web presses that turn out the big dailies are shrinking, and with that comes the width of the paper.

The standard for a long time has been the 54-inch web. Now the 50-inch web is considered the new standard, but the same wide pages can't be printed on the 50-inch. The Guardian was recently redesigned to the smaller Berliner format (about 12.25" wide) to fit two spreads side-by-side when printed on the 50-inch. The Toronto Star is almost a quarter-inch wider than the redesigned Guardian. Broadsheets are traditionally closer to 15", but have been shrinking for decades.

In the 1960s, most broadsheets were 15" wide, printed on the 60-inch web. Yet it's the page's length that makes all the difference. Tabloids are themselves around 11.5" wide, an inch away from the more respectable broadsheet. However, most tabs stop at 14–17" in length and the broadsheet continues to 22 or 23". The Berliner format goes to about 18.5" in length, a good four inches less than a standard broadsheet. The Guardian has had great success with the new format—increased circulation, positive reader response and Society for News Design awards.

What does the 50-inch web mean to student newspapers right now? Probably very little, unless your paper is printed on the same web press that a big city daily is printed. Then again, your printer will want to keep up with the industry that's sticking to one standard. One press width means every printer buys the same width of paper, making it easier to produce. At some point, your printer may switch to a 50-inch web. This will affect a few broadsheet student newspapers, which may have to go thinner and redesign in the process. As for the tabloid papers out there, their length or width could change. Tabloids are normally half the size of a broadsheet and mostly printed sideways—eight pages versus the broadsheet's four. While a broadsheet will be squeezed thinner, the same change will cause the tabloid's length to be shortened.

Student newspapers have the opportunity to reshape both the way news is covered and the graphic style in which it's done. Some see the 50-inch as a step toward the more reader-friendly tabloid. Most student papers print on tabs, making them the testing ground for new ideas and design. If the future of newspapers is on tabloids, the student press can innovate the tab and be a learning ground for journalists who will eventually work in a tabloid world. ■

1.3 Terms

Agate: a unit of measurement for the length of a page used especially for advertising. 14 agate lines equal 1 column-inch or 5.5 points per agate.

Barker: a reversed-out kicker or flag, placed above a headline with a short phrase. Eg. "Extra", "Exclusive", "Breaking news".

Baseline: the horizontal line on which the bottom of most type is aligned—with the exception of letters with descenders (p,q,j).

Berliner: named for the Berliner Zeitung newspaper, this unique size is a result of a smaller press width over the broadsheet. The Berliner measures about 12.5" wide by 18.25" tall, making it slightly wider than a tabloid.

Blackletter: often called Old English or textura, a family of type drawn with a broad stroke to match early written manuscripts. Once quite popular for a newspaper's nameplate.

Bleed: printing an image beyond the edge of a page—the image is printed larger and trimmed to have the ink appear to extend to the page or sheet edge.

Broadsheet: the broadsheet paper denotes the newspaper folded in half with a traditionally serious sensibility. A large sheet of paper with information printed on one side defines the broadside that evolved into the modern broadsheet.

Camera-ready: copy (type and art) that is ready to be photographed.

Caption: line of type for illustration / photo, also called overline or cutline.

Center spread: the two pages at the center of a newspaper or section where artwork and text can bleed across as one page. Also called a double truck.

CMYK: the subtractive process colors: cyan, magenta, yellow and black used to create a full range of colors. Newspapers usually have more Black (K) only pages then full-color or CMYK pages.

Color separation: the process of separating color original artwork into the four-process color plates.

Color swatch: a sample of a particular ink or blend, similar to a paint chip—the printer will match the ink you choose to their swatch.

Continuous tone: an image that contains gradient tones from black to white.

Cursive: a typeface that resembles handwriting but not tied together as a Script typeface is.

Deck: that section of a subhead composed of one or more lines usually set below a headline. Also called a subhead or kicker.

Double truck: two newspaper pages that are treated as a single unit. A photo or article may be spread across two pages side-by-side, most likely with a gutter between unless it is a centre spread.

Dot gain: a defect in which dots print larger than they should, causing darker tones or stronger colors. Newsprint absorbs and spreads ink, guaranteeing some dot gain.

Em: the square of any type at size, approximately the width of an uppercase "M". An em-dash (—) is a dash also the width of an "M" used to break out a separate thought within a sentence. Option-Shift-minus in any Mac application—however, Word will replace with an en-dash. Em can also refer to a space in type of the same width.

En: half the width of an em in the same typeface, the width of an uppercase "N". An en-dash (–) is used to separate a range of numbers such as a date, eg. 1999–2004. Option-minus will pull it up in any Mac application.

EPS: encapsulated postscript, a file format used to transfer graphic images between compatible applications, especially vector artwork, fonts and duotone images.

Flag: another word for nameplate (see nameplate). Also a line of type, separate from but within, an article categorizing the article. Eg. "Campus News", "Music", "Book Review".

Folio: a line that gives a newspaper's name and the page number.

Font: a complete alphabet with figures and symbols, originally all in one size and style as lead type.

Form: the assembly of pages for printing—each side of a grouping represents a form.

Gothic: a description for sans serif typefaces commonly designed for newspapers. The term Gothic or Grotesk is an earlier name for the modern sans serif typeface.

Hairline: the thinnest rule (or line) in layout software that will print.

Headline: a line of text set usually at the top of an article calling attention to the story—considered the main entry point into a story. Abbreviated as head.

Halftone: the reproduction of a continuous tone image, through a process of capturing a screened photograph, which converts the image into dots.

Imposition: the positioning of pages on forms so that after printing, folding and cutting, all pages will be in proper sequence.

Ink absorption: the amount of ink a particular paper stock will absorb on the printing press.

Jump head: a small headline or phrase over a story continued from a different page.

Justification: the alignment of type. Flush-left refers to type aligned left and ragged right (rag right). Flush-right/rag left would be the reverse. Justified type is flush-left and flush-right.

Kerning: the adjustment of space between characters of type, in order to fix awkward spacing.

Kicker: a short line in smaller type set below the headline. Also called a subhead. Also considered a teaser, eyebrow, highline and over-line when referred to a line of text "above the main deck of a head" (Arnold, 332).

Leading: lines of white space between lines of type calculated as the total height the takes up. Eg. 12-point type with 15-point leading (written 12/15) consists of 3-points of leading added to the 12-points for the type making a total of 15-points.

Ligature: type characters consisting of two or more united letters, such as fi, ffi and fl. The non-joined characters are set too close and the strokes overlap.

Lines per inch (lpi): the number of lines of dots in an inch as reproduced on the printing press—also called the linescreen.

Loupe: an optical lens used for inspecting proofs, photographs and printing.

M: an abbreviation printers use for a quantity of 1,000. A 10,000 run of newspapers would also be 10 M.

Masthead: the printed statement of name, ownership, staff and contact information of a newspaper.

Moiré: the unwanted screen pattern caused by incorrect screen angles or scanning a printed image without descreening.

Nameplate: the name of the newspaper as a logo on the front page. Also called a flag or banner. Often incorrectly called a masthead.

Offset: an indirect printing process where ink is transferred to a substrate (paper) from a blanket (a rubber wrapped roller) that carries an impression from the printing plate—instead of directly from the printing plate.

Over-banner: a headline or teaser above the nameplate. Also called a skyline.

PDF: portable document file format used for the transfer of designs, the PDF is considered a universal file format, built using postscript and is device and resolution independent.

Pica: a unit of measurement for the height and width of any graphic element, especially type. One pica is equal to 12 points, and 6 picas equal 1 inch. Picas and points are written: 1p6 or 1 pica and 6 points.

Pilcrow: the name of the paragraph symbol (¶), used as a hidden character in layout software to represent the paragraph break, also used for reference or as an editing mark.

Point: a unit of measurement used for type and leading heights as well as line or rule thickness. Points are also smaller units to measure between picas.

PostScript: a page description language created by Adobe to describe an image for printing in a purely text-based format. Most laser printers use postscript to reproduce the image.

Process colours: the four colors CMYK that make up the subtractive primary colors used in printing.

Pull-quote: a quote or excerpt pulled from an article and set in larger type to act as a teaser.

Register: the exact alignment of two of more printing images (separated colors) to reproduce the full-color image.

Rule: a solid or styled line measured in points used to separate articles.

Saddle stitch: the method of binding where a booklet is fastened at the fold with staples or wire.

Screen angles: the angles at which the halftone screens are place in relation to one another to avoid unwanted moiré patterns. In process printing the angles used are, cyan 105°, magenta 75°, yellow 90° and black 45°.

Script: any typeface that is drawn like handwriting and joined together somewhat seamlessly.

Signature: a multi-page printed sheet of paper after it has been cut and folded. One sheet of newsprint holding two 2-sided pages is a signature. A 16-page paper with 4-pages per signature would therefore have 4 signatures. Multiple signatures would have been printed together, each side of which is a form (see form).

Skybox: the teaser box or boxes above the nameplate advertising other sections or articles.

Skyline: short for skyline banner, a line of text above the nameplate, part of the skybox.

Spot color: printing a second color in addition to black. The spot color is usually pre-mixed ink used for exact color matching.

Square serif: also known as slab serif, a roman typeface with slab or square serifs. Usually the thickness of the stroke and the serifs is equal.

Subtractive primaries: the hues used in process printing: cyan, magenta and yellow.

Tabloid: used to describe both a smaller-format half of a broadsheet, as well as a type of journalism considered less serious and more sensational than in a broadsheet. Tabloids are restricted widthwise (about 11 inches depending on the press) to any length (though usually 12 to 18 inches).

Tone: the shade, hue or degree of lightness of a color.

Web offset: an offset press in which a roll of paper is fed into a press and printed on both sides in one continuous pass (or web). Newspapers are printed on web presses, which can print several two-sided multiple color pages and output a trimmed and folded paper in one pass.

STEP TWO
DESIGN

2.0 Introduction

Designing a newspaper has a few steps. Whether beginning from a redesign or evolving an existing design, this section offers a basic understanding on how to use design in a newspaper. An editor or designer new to their paper's current design may find the information relevant to understanding how the paper arrived at its graphic style. Each element on page exists for a reason and understanding the reasons leads to better design.

There are several ways to go through a redesign: in one quick rush or in slow progressive steps. Normally there is a lot of work behind the scenes preparing the new design and new templates — this may or may not happen when new software is installed.

Some papers only need a few improvements. These can be done in increments, changing a few elements each issue with little notice by the reader. In general, newsreaders have been a conservative group uncomfortable with change, so after a redesign, one might expect both positive and negative feedback. However, readers are becoming savvy to good design and can accept large redesigns more frequently then in the past. The more drastic the change, the more work the reader will have to perform to find their favorite section. Designs are easier to change then the location of the Sudoku.

When it comes to a rush redesign, make sure to have an experienced designer — or read this book — and expect to work out the bugs over a few editions. Even done quickly, a good redesign can have a lasting positive effect on a newspaper.

2.1 News Page Basics

As you begin to assemble your newspaper design you need to have the right tools at your disposal: graphic and text elements that build each page. Consider these the foundation on which each page is laid out—the underlying structure is formed by the grid.

The previous step laid out a foundation of basic building blocks—literally. Step 2 looks at the mechanics of each element and illustrates how these can be applied to the design of a newspaper. Where Step 1 was the blocks being moved around to build a page, Step 2 is the content within those blocks—not the news, but the finer elements on each page. Designing a page with a hierarchy, visual dominance and contrast may not be effective with poor typesetting and a weak page foundation.

These principles are universal to design and in this section they will be applied to news design.

2.1.1 GRID

The page's grid is a simple structure with a lot of potential, while a large daily broadsheet paper may appear to use 6 columns per page, often the paper uses more that you don't see. A tabloid paper may only use 5 columns.

Consider increasing the number of columns to create flexibility. The example here has a 21-column grid—an odd number of columns are used to ensure there is always a spare column. The grid for this paper began as a 5-column page, but was multiplied by 4 to get the flexibility of a grid that allowed for 4 or 5 columns to be combined—pages vary between 4 and 5 columns depending on the purpose.

2.1.2 COLUMNS

A newspaper's design should have flexibility with the choice of column width. There are two considerations when approaching column width choice: the type of information being presented, and controlling readability for the reader.

The width of a standard column is determined by the reading speed, the type size and typeface chosen. The general rule for set-

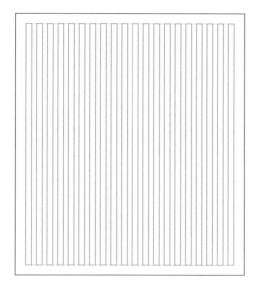

Grid and colums: a 5-column grid is standard for a tabloid (right), but a 20-column grid can be more flexible (left).

ting type in a column for perfect reading width and proper spacing is to multiply the point size in picas by two—10 point type would then be 20 picas or 3.33 inches. Average news columns run around 2 inches wide, which fall well under the perfect width, but still within a comfortable range. Dropping to 1.5 inches or below will create columns too narrow for justified text—flush left being preferable in such narrow columns—because the tight column width of a justified column will create large gaps between words.

Due to the length of news paragraphs—short paragraphs broken after a sentence or two—wide columns will have large spaces left at the end of most paragraphs which is unsightly and decreases readability. Leave wider columns to feature articles with longer paragraphs.

The graphic style of a newspaper should allow switching between a few column width options (see 2.1.1 Grid). Such switching can match content—the type of news—and create contrast between several articles on one page.

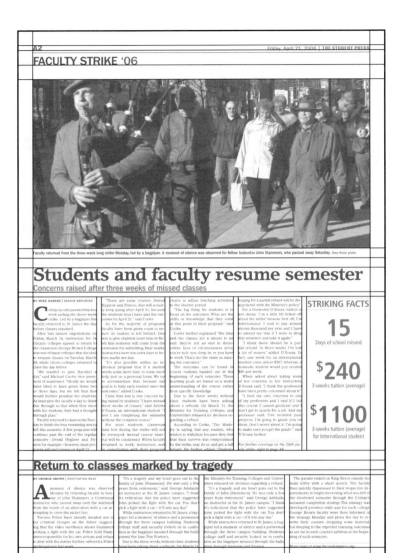

Vary the columns: a news page, 12.25" x 18.375". the column width is varied between the two stories. the fifth column on the top article has been used for a small info-graphic.

COLUMN WIDTH

7/9, width 7 pica

Imagine turning on your television today to find you only have one channel to watch and for some reason, it's in black and white. Not so long ago Canadian viewers had very few channels to watch — three in most cities — and cable was not yet popular as it offered no better choice.

The first Canadian television broadcast began with a news item hosted by Lorne Green — before he left Canada to star in the American western drama Bonanza. Television in Canada started in 1952 with one network broadcasting in English and French, the Canadian Broadcasting Corporation (CBC)/ Société Radio-

7/9, width 14 pica

Canada (SRC). Only Canadians could watch the CBC in Toronto and Montreal that first year, but by 1955 the CBC/Radio-Canada had expanded to reach 66 per cent of the Canadian population.

The CBC/ Radio-Canada enjoyed nine years dominating the Canadian airwaves, although there had always been American broadcast signals sneaking across the border. In 1961 the CTV Network began broadcasting, at the permission of the CBC — which meant they created their own competition. The CBC controlled broadcasting in Canada until the Canadian Radio-Television Commission (CRTC) was established in 1968.

In the early days of the CRTC, the rules governing Canadian television were established, including granting licenses and controlling amounts of Canadian content. 1970 brought the first content regulations making sure that all TV broadcasters in Canada had to fill their schedules with at least 60 per cent Canadian content.

Television grew slightly in the 1970s with the first private French-language network, TVA in 1971 and Global in 1974—as well as educational channels TV Ontario, Access Alberta and B.C.'s Knowledge network. In 1972, Toronto also saw the launch of City-TV which has served as the base for many more channels.

Fewer and wider columns will slow the reader down slightly, making the reader spend more time digesting the information. A column too narrow or too wide will also slow the reader down, but by decreasing readability.

2.2 Type Basics

Type in many ways deserves its own section—or even a book. Below is a brief understanding of type in designing the news page. There are a few basics concerning type that are worth knowing before using type in the newspaper design.

Robert Bringhurst's *The Elements of Typographic Style* is the definitive stylebook on the subject of type and typesetting—including the proper way to use characters of typographic importance outside the standard alphabet such as the umlaut (ö) or pilcrow

(¶). An authority on typography, Bringhurst is also a noted Canadian poet, author and linguist who has studied, translated and written on Haida myth tellers. Typography is expressed through Bringhurst as an art form with substantial historical context.

2.2.1 READABILITY VS. LEGIBILITY

Most of this discussion on type will revolve around readability, which is controlled through choices the designer makes, such as point size (see 2.2.7), leading (see 2.2.8) and line length (see 2.1.2). The typeface's designer determines legibility. The design drew the letterforms, making an interpretation on the basic form of the alphabet. The reader then needs to be able to recognize these interpretations as the normal letterform. Typefaces such as script, blackletter or novelty fonts may not be as easy to recognize because the reader is less familiar with the forms and must think slightly longer to interpret the word.

Blackletter was the typeface of choice for Gutenburg because it matched the lettering in books of the era. Now readers struggle to recognize letters that don't look like standard Roman lettering. Roman serif letters even edge out sans serif letters, which without the serifs, become harder to read. Crafting a serif letter is a delicate operation to archive a unique letter that still reads as that letter. Imagine if we only had one subject for painting—the Mona Lisa—and all paintings are based on recreating the face, but with subtle changes to the smile or eyes, but most the painting would have to be recognized as a Mona Lisa.

A reader's eye moves along a line of text, taking in a few letters before jumping to another grouping. In that split second, the brain must recognize those letters before moving on. Poor legibility makes the reader pause to think, and the reader may not recover from that loss in speed as they continue through the text. The brain processes the top half of a line of text more thoroughly, making it therefore important that the letter "h" not read "n" because the ascender is too short.

Readability is easily controlled by the designer, who can set type in a line of optimum length with the right point size and space between the lines. See 2.2.3 for further discussion surrounding typeface choice.

Parts of the character

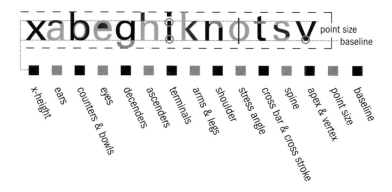

2.2.2 PARTS OF THE CHARACTER AND LANGUAGE

Metal type had a profound effect on the language we use to describe type and typesetting. Movable type, mostly made from lead or wood, has been used for over five centuries and is now popular among artisan printers and hobbyists rather than commercial printers. Typesetting itself was originally the act of compositing a page from the individual characters—type was set into a chase, the frame the type was locked into. A typesetter had only a few typefaces to choose from because of the limitations of having to stock enough characters for each. Type was stored in drawers with individual compartments for each character. Each typeface would be split between two drawers—the upper case stored capital letters we now call the uppercase, and the lower case stored what is now lowercase letters.

The face of any movable type character is wrong-reading—as with a rubber stamp, the pressed image is right-reading. A typesetter would take the individual wrong-reading characters one at a time and place them on a composing stick, which was a hand-held ledge that had a movable guard to control the column width. A line of text was usually measured out first to determine the required spaces and where the last word broke. This process, much like putting a puzzle together, was time consuming and required attention to avoid mistakes.

Typesetting required adjustments to space type to fit or for better reading. Between lines of type, a thin strip of lead about one point high was inserted to create what we now call leading. Typesetting is now done using computers, without the physical contact or control lead type had. Yet the foundation of type came from the days of movable type. While the language remains, the meaning has changed slightly.

2.2.3   TYPEFACE CHOICE:

Choosing the right typeface (also called a font) can be difficult, and is very much a combination of aesthetics and function. The typeface has to work by being legible and reproducing on newsprint. As well, the typeface should look good and appealing to the eye. Each letter in a font has been carefully formed and yet when printed at 9 point in a sentence, the individual character's unique shape should not stand out. A good typeface is one that the reader doesn't notice.

The typeface's designer made legibility decisions. There are a number of typefaces that are designed for the best legibility while being slightly condensed, yet also for printing on newsprint at high speeds. Mercury, Miller or Gulliver typefaces fill those specifications.

In choosing a typeface for body text, the general rule is to use a serif typeface. Using the wrong typeface for extended blocks of text will make reading harder, tiring the reader, or even shortening the hold the reader will have on the block of text. In his book Type and Layout, Colin Wheildon describes studies that have shown that readers are more than five times likelier to comprehend a block of text when a serif typeface is used instead of a sans serif typeface.

Such studies reflect a reality in North America, where readers have not adopted the use of sans serif body text. Even in Europe, it's found mostly in magazines rather than newspapers. However, with the increase in screen reading from websites and the slow increase in newspapers focused on short news bites over lengthy articles, the North American reader may soon become more comfortable with the use of a sans serif for text font.

The use of a sans serif typeface is helpful in creating contrast between elements. A page using serif type exclusively wouldn't have the same impact as a page using both sans and serif typefaces. Type size, color and case also help the elements contrast. (See 2.2.10 Using Type)

Narrowing the body text choice to serif typefaces only may feel restrictive with little variation between faces. How many variations on the basic letterform of each character in the alphabet can there really be?

Thousands, actually, all with minor differences one would only see under a magnifying loupe. The decorative details are one variation, but there are others that affect the typeface's fitting. When setting the same block of type using several typefaces in a side-by-side comparison, the variations become more apparent. The strength of the type on the page—also called type color—the width of the character and x-height can affect the overall spacing of the text block.

When choosing the correct typefaces for your paper, have several varying weights within a font family. Times Regular, Times

Sample Typefaces

Serif

abcdefghij
Corona 24pt

abcdefghij
Excelsior 24pt

abcdefghij
Nimrod 24pt

abcdefghij
Times Europa 24pt

abcdefghij
Utopia 24pt

Sans Serif

abcdefghij
Bell Gothic 24pt

abcdefghij
ITC Franklin Gothic 24pt

abcdefghij
Frutiger 24pt

abcdefghij
News Gothic 24pt

abcdefghij
Trade Gothic 24pt

Italic, Times Bold and Times Bold Italic are all different weights and styles in the Times family.

Assuming your paper doesn't have a budget for more typefaces, do a search on the office computers for any previous fonts. Your campus computer store may also sell Adobe's Type Collection for educational customers fairly cheaply. There are a few websites devoted to typefaces, such as www.myfonts.com, or should you like a typeface already printed somewhere, www.identifont.com will help you give it a name.

Consider the following characteristics when choosing the typefaces for your newspaper:
- Legibility
- Ability to survive the printing press
- Range of weights within a family

A FEW OF THE FACES IN THE NEIGHBORHOOD:

The typeface gracing the pages of USA Today is Gulliver, a serif face designed for newsprint. Those familiar with reading some of the Canadian national dailies will not necessarily know the names of their typefaces. Utopia serves as the body text for The Globe and Mail, and Walbaum—also known as Walburn—for headlines. At The National Post, Miller is used for body text and headlines. Both papers had a type designer create a custom typeface or customize an existing face. Not all papers use custom newspaper fonts, though. Montreal's Le Devoir uses Century Old Style for its headlines and body text, with a mix of Torino and Industrial. The Toronto Star redesigned in 2002 and made the change from Times Roman to a custom face, Torstar.

Thanks to its near ubiquitous presence on all computers, Times Roman is not considered a serious typeface. However, developed in 1932, Times Roman (or more often called Times New Roman) was briefly a proprietary font in metal type for The Times of London. It quickly became popular in metal form released by Monotype and again with the advent of Postscript and laser printers. It is a newspaper typeface and The Times has since updated their in-house version of Times many, er, times. Times Europa is the 1970s update, followed by other versions including Times Millennium and now Times Classic.

2.2.4 **SERIF AND SANS SERIF TYPE**

Typefaces fall under a few categories based on their general characteristics of shape. A typeface is often referred to by its category: modern, transitional, novelty, script, slab serif and sans serif. The two most important categories are serif and sans serif. Serif type has small decorative strokes off of the end of a letter's main strokes that improve readability and guide the reader down the line of type. Sans means "without" in French, thus sans serif is type without serifs.

2.2.5 **X-HEIGHT**

A typeface's x-height is a measure of the height of the lowercase x. This height will be consistent for most other lowercase letters so that the height of the x is the same as the height of the "a" or "m". The x-height is also a portion of the total height of a typeface and varies. Some typefaces have larger x-heights and their lowercase letters are closer in size to their uppercase letters.

The trend with typefaces specifically designed for newspapers is toward larger x-heights, which makes the type at the same point size appear larger, which in turn helps improve readability. Recent newspaper designs among dailies have yielded visually larger text type yet a tighter fit, which allows more letters per line and increases the total words per page.

Comparing x-heights

abcd xT abcd xT

Minion Pro 30pt   Corona 30pt

2.2.6 **TYPE HEIGHT AND WIDTH**

No two typefaces are exactly the same. Fonts vary by the same details in the serifs or by their height or width. Many typefaces specifically designed for newspapers are narrow to fit more letters in the tight news columns. The x-height and its portion of the total height may make one typeface look large than another.

Below is an explanation of how to choose type and it's important to remember that with each typeface comes a bit of tweaking to arrive at the right setting for point size. Avoid using the vertical and horizontal controls that alter the height and width of characters—this is done by stretching or compressing the type and causes the type strokes and curves to be out of proportion.

2.2.7 TYPEFACE SIZE

The preferred size of body text and other text elements is determined by readability, the particular typeface and type-element contrast. For example, body text is set between 8 and 10 points and depends on the size of the letters at any point size—some type looks bigger at 10 point than another might. The text also needs to be large enough to be readable while not being so big that the column is too narrow.

2.2.8 LEADING

Lines of type are spaced out by leading (rhymes with heading) based on traditional typesetting with metal type, where a set of characters came in a point size and zero leading. To increase space between lines, thin stripes of lead were inserted, its thickness measured by the point. With computers, leading determines the total height of each line. Nine points of text over 11 points leading is an 11 point line height rather than 11 points between lines.

Using leading to space lines of type improves readability and reading speed. Not enough leading will make text feel too tight and the reader cramped—focusing on a particular line is made harder. Too much leading in news design opens up the page and takes away from the solid look a page of text can have.

2.2.9 TESTING TYPE

As mentioned above, in order to choose the appropriate typeface, it needs to be tested. Use a portion of a previously published articles set in one column and repeat the same block of text, each with a different typeface. Comparing several typefaces along with weight variations on the same typeface will help make a decision on the correct body text font. Start by setting those different typefaces at the same point size. Choose 9 points for the text and allow InDesign or Quark to set "Auto" as the leading. Print out the example and read it. When reviewing the copy, see whether it is comfortable and easy to read through. Show it to others to read.

Comparing several typefaces can help you make a decision on a favorite. Now print another mockup with each column set in a different point size — and leading either on "Auto" or 2–3 points more than the body text. Often the right point size for the body text is between two full points — 8.7 points or 9.5 points. It's worth some experimentation to find the right size; however, even after choosing a point size and using it in an issue of your paper, you can adjust it. This is especially true once you see the type printed on the regular newsprint stock by your printer.

When creating the mockups of the new design, lay out a full page or two with real articles and photographs. Most layout applications have filler text that is not real prose. It is better to use text that your paper will actually print or has printed because you want to be able to read the example as a real news story.

LEADING

11/11
Imagine turning on your television today to find you only have one channel to watch and for some reason, it's in black and white. Not so long ago Canadian viewers had very few channels to watch — three in most cities — and cable was not yet popular as it offered no better choice.

11/15
Imagine turning on your television today to find you only have one channel to watch and for some reason, it's in black and white. Not so long ago Canadian viewers had very few channels to watch — three in most cities — and cable was not yet popular as it offered no better choice.

While this was only a lesson in choosing a body text, the paper will also need a typeface for headlines, pull-quotes, bylines, photo captions and credits, folios and sidebars. With just one body text or a few—no more than three—lay out mockups with a pair of fonts, the body text and a compatible sans serif. Mix up the combination to vary the choices. Again, when looking for a complementary font, look for a typeface family with varied weights and styles—or even more than the body text. The body text chosen may have a family style for headlines (also called display) or the medium or bold style might work well here. A typeface that is condensed or even slightly narrower is preferable for the headline font as it will allow the maximum number of letters to fit the space while still being large enough to stand out.

2.2.10 USING TYPE

Finally before advancing to the next step, consider how type is used on the news page.. Type does not need to only be set in sentence case or Title Case. USE ALL CAPS FOR BYLINES OR ARTICLE FLAGS. Use color to separate the sub-headline from the headline. And of course, the size of type used will help create contrast between text elements. There is more information later in this section that covers useful typesetting techniques.

2.3 Text Elements

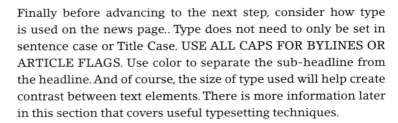

With the palette of typefaces chosen for your publication, the next step is to decide how those typefaces will be applied to the text elements on each page and which typeface will be used for elements that haven't yet been identified.

STYLES FOR HEADLINES, SUBHEAD AND BYLINES

A newspaper's design can look good over time by keeping the overall design consistent. With a few typefaces chosen for your newspaper, decide how and when to use each typeface. News designers often refer to the design as architecture—the page is constructed in a specific way with a hierarchy of information and an underlying structure, without which pages would be a cluttered mess. Using the same typeface for every element on the page will diminish the chance of contrast between elements, creating a sea of sameness on the page. The size and shape of text elements can help them stand apart, yet as these items have similarities (the same two typefaces) and are consistent (the graphic style) throughout, the system works together. You are creating a visual system of interchangeable parts that vary based on their need.

2.3.1 HEADLINES

Except for front-page news, the headline doesn't need to sell the reader on that particular paper, but it does need to entice the reader into that article. Even with a well-worded, witty or clever headline, few readers will be pulled in if it has been poorly set.

When beginning a redesign, consider finding more than one way to enter an article and build a collection for the paper's graphic style. There are the usual headline and graphic, but there are other eye-catching and information-filled cues for the reader.

There should be two or more styles of headline. Create one headline style to be used with a sub-headline, another for use with a deck and still another for secondary articles without either a sub-headline or deck. The visual identity of the paper should also allow for headlines in sidebars that may or may not be miniatures of the regular headlines.

Choose a style for setting the headline—centered, flush left with white space on the right or justified to fit across the entire width of the article. A few old styles dating back to the 1950s— and still used in the New York Times—had headlines stacked in pyramids or stepped. These were popular for multi-line few column headlines and would take up a great deal of space if used over several columns.

Headline setting is often a matter of taste. Some designers swear by having a headline not only justified to fit, but also written to fit across the article—going as far to say that the journalist wasn't doing their job by having a headline that was too short. Yet flush left headlines look better and allow breathing room rather then a crammed page.

Students and facul

Concerns raised after three weeks of mis

BY MIKE BARKER | SENIOR REPORTER   "There are some courses, Dental   chairs to adju
                                      Hygiene and Fitness, that will actu- the shorter pe

Headline styles: these two headlines appear on the same page. The example above shows a headline and contrasting sub-head, set in the serif (Lino Letter at 43pt) and sans serif (Franklin Gothic Book at 22pt). Below is a secondary headline set in Franklin Gothic Demi at 30pt. While the two styles use the same set of typefaces, the difference creates contrast between what could be too similar elements. There is also a sizing difference between the two headlines, while the secondary headline is still larger than the sub-head above.

Return to classes marked by t

BY GEORGE BROWN | EDUCTATION BEAT   deal with the matter further, inferred a   lege staff and

Headlines can also be set in uppercase, title case with most words capitalized or regular sentence case. The amount of capitalization usually relates to the voice your paper uses when speaking to the reader—a sentence case headline is less formal then title case. Uppercase headlines should have extra tracking or kerning—space between letters—as the reader's eye normally looks for the top half of letters to read a line, which is easier with the greater variation in lowercase letters.

The practice of underlining headlines was abandoned in the 50s with the exception of a few newspapers. Punctuation is exactly that and should be used carefully to punctuate on those rare special occasions. When in doubt, follow the Canadian Press style guide.

Finally the paper's graphic style should allow for a hierarchy of headlines, which will allow setting articles in order of importance. A flexible system with multiple typeface weights and sizes as well as a mix of one serif display and one sans serif font to mix and match, will keep a page of headlines looking different—helping the reader distinguish the various articles.

2.3.2 SUB-HEADLINES / DECKS

When using a sub-headline (also called a deck or kick), the key is contrast between it and the headline. Employ color, case, style, size, and type category to make the sub-headline distinct enough. While size variation is almost a given, use at least two other characteristics to vary the text, such as using a sans serif sub-headline in 70 per cent black to counter the serif solid black headline. Setting the sub-head in the same typeface as the headline with little other differences may distract readers into reading it as one sentence rather than two.

The setting for the sub-head should also match the headline or be completely separate. A centered or flush-left headline should have a sub-head in the same alignment or be set in another location entirely, such as in the first few lines in the article.

Subhead: while long headlines should be avoided, more information can be given in a subhead (or a deck). The one above is set with a 70% black screen for contrast, as well a sans serif typeface is used against the serif headline. In this example, the subhead is paired with the headline, rather than sitting into the copy block below it. Below a deck is set below the headline, embedded into the copy block.

2.3.3 BYLINE

Again having more than one style allows for interchangeable design depending on the purpose. Take one or two typefaces that you chose for the paper and create a number of styles—at least one for the serif and one for the sans serif font.

Short news bites, CD review and snippets of text hardly need to lead with a prominent byline. Instead, have a style for a short byline at the end of the article. Be slightly playful with the regular byline—it may still be indented into the text or float outside the text block as a separate element and it should be flexible for bylines with editorial titles or wire credits. The paper may also want another style for editorials or columns.

Aside from the option of placing the byline at the beginning or end of the main body text, the byline can be written into the deck, sit as a separate element between the headline and body text blocks, or accompany a photo in box.

Byline: the two examples above show the style embedded into the copy block between the subhead and the main copy. Below are two examples where the byline is placed at the end of the article, especially useful for short copy such as reviews, news bites and letters.

2.3.4 SIDEBARS:

Running sidebars in a different typeface is an excellent way to separate the sidebar from the main text. Often what might be called a sidebar is another article or piece of information entirely separate and should have a look to identify it as such. The sidebar should also have its own headline style that comes from the selection of headline styles already created. Use one of the bylines from the established system.

Sidebar: often two related articles are placed together, but to separate them, one is set in a secondary body typeface. News bites, background and event listings work well set in a sans serif which helps the page not be entirely serif body text. As sans serif type takes slightly longer to recognize, it's best used in shorter articles.

2.3.5 PULL-QUOTES:

Add a text element to articles by pulling a quote or phrase from an article. Avoid using pull-quotes as filler, but rather as a teaser. The pull-quote needs to be distinctly different when surrounded by body text and near a headline. Even a heavier weight or italics variation on the body text typeface will make a good pull-quote style. Set the pull-quote larger than the body text but smaller than the headline, which needs to remain larger for dominance.

The pull-quote style can also use large grey quotation marks (or another unique character) with a rule or two depending on the paper's graphic style. A pull-quote is a separate element that should be read outside the normal flow of the article. Avoid turning a paragraph in the main body text into a pull-quote as the reader is unlikely to read the quoted paragraph in sequence.

> ur remaining weeks / few programs will end of the regular Hygiene and Fit- however, most pro- ses on April 21. he courses, Dental ss, that will actual- r April 21, because have met the out- " said Cooke. ority of programs given room to en- s left behind. One ts more time to fin- will come from the nitting final marks. n extra days to be- . ble within an in-
>
> three weeks of classes," said Arlette D'Souza, an international student. "I feel I am completing the semester without the complete course."
> For most students, classroom time lost during the strike will not be recouped; instead course mate- rial will be condensed. When faculty returned to work, instructors met in consultation with their program chairs to adjust teaching activities to the shorter period.
> "The big thing for students is to focus on the outcomes. What are the skills or knowledge that they need at this point in their program," said Cooke.
> Cooke further explained "the time and the classes are a means to an end; they're not an end in them-
> understanding of the course, rather then specific knowledge.
>
> ❝ **The big thing for students is to focus on the outcomes. What are the skills or knowledge that they need at this point in their pro- gram,"** said Cooke.
>
> Due to the three weeks without class, students have been asking about a refunds. On March 31, the Ministry for Training, Colleges and
> hoping for appointed For a fru not cheap. about the s internation eleven thou to extend this semest "I think tial refund a lot of m fact, one w student co domestic s $80 per we When a of her cor D'Souza sa have been

Pull-quote: while breaking the body text, this pull-quote is designed to read separately.

2.3.6 PHOTO CAPTIONS/CREDITS:

Many times a photo is run as an article. Allegedly worth a thousand words, the photo may not speak for itself, even when accompanied by an article. Photo captions are used to explain the photo and as with any other text element, use a typeface that contrasts against the body text. Consider that the photo and caption may need to stand-alone and the style can therefore be similar to the sidebar or information box (see below).

If you use a good amount of staff photos, talk to your photographer to get photos with extra space for captions or negative space (blank wall or sky)—especially for feature photos. There are many creative and interesting ways to add the caption.

With the caption comes the photo credit and the placement decision. The photo credit traditionally is set in 5 or 6-point type, but that doesn't have to be the case. Place the photo credit where it seems best—along the side, ending the caption, photo corner.

Faculty returned from the three-week long strike Monday, led by a bagpiper. A mom

Photo caption: will describe and offer context for the photo.

DESIGN · REQUIRES ASSEMBLY

2.3.7   INFORMATION BOXES

While sidebars may range from an entire article to a list of details, some articles may have one piece of information to be highlighted. Often articles end with a short note with the website or email address, but previews can contain the event details, separate from the article's body. Possibly there is one small fact that can be pulled out not as a pull-quote, but rather as a point form note. In these cases, using an information box is useful and another helpful way to present the key information.

Create a style that contrasts the regular body text and fits within the whole graphic style. Aside from the typography style, add additional graphic elements—rules, boxes, or a large "i" information icon. The info box style can be designed to be scalable and used in several ways—possibly as a modified pull-quote or as a small sidebar.

Info-box: an info box can present a few facts, that help the story, not included in the main text. This is example is thin to avoid poor text wrapping in the adjacent columns.

2.3.8   OTHER ELEMENTS

There are a number of other text elements yet to be explored in this section, including folios/page headers (described in 2.4.6), jumps and flags. With any additional text elements, follow the graphic style already set for the publication. Of these three extra elements, none need be typeset in a typeface other than the two already chosen. There is a lot of flexibility when choosing two families of typefaces. More options in one typeface increase the chances of having variation in the graphic style. Using a series of condensed width typefaces from the same family for one part of the paper and the regular width variations for another part still allows for consistency. While these typefaces will vary, each was designed together, making them interchangeable.

Finally with all the styles set for each text element, refer to 2.5 Template and Styleguide to lock the styles in.

> **THE STUDENT PRESS** | Friday, April 21, 2006   **A3**
> # FACULTY STRIKE '06

Headers, folios & flags: the newspaper's graphic style can allow for a simple system or a more detailed header. The folio (often with the date and publication) might even placed at the bottom of the page, leaving the header alone at the top.

2.4   Design Elements

So far in the newspaper design process, type has served as the basic building blocks of the news page. The use of type adds contrast, texture and to a small degree, structure. The page needs structure, as well as consistency from page to page. There are a few design elements that can be used on the page to build structure on the single page and throughout the entire publication. These elements are fundamental to laying out the news page in order to serve or reach the reader.

2.4.1   PAGE HIERARCHY

Each page of the newspaper should have a structured hierarchy where each element has an order of importance. There is always a top story that will get the prominent position, usually at the top of the page. While there is still a hierarchy from the front cover to the back, each page must have a similar structure.

Early in the design process of creating a mockup, show clear examples of pages where the reader's eye would be given a focal point—the dominant article—and guided to the successive articles. Using size, shape and the bag of design tricks (contrast, white space) the important article will draw the reader's eye—even if the reader then skips to the next article.

North American readers read left to right, top to bottom; the most important information may then be near the top. However, placing all emphasis on the top article may cause the page to feel top heavy and will need balance. A graphic element such as a photo, pull-quote, sidebar or graphic will break up the grey text and give the bottom an anchor.

2.4.2 DOMINANT ELEMENT

On any page there not only should be a hierarchy, but one item should stand out the most. A photo, graphic or headline should be the largest, most dominant element compared to all others. Without a dominant graphic, use a headline, but set the type at least twice as large as any other headline on that page.

2.4.3 GRAPHIC ELEMENTS

A page cannot survive on text alone. There are a number of ways to add simple elements to the page design even before the use of photography and graphics. Each text element is already a graphic element that builds the page to the final composition. Using those text elements differently and with style, can actually accomplish the same effect as non-text graphic elements, such as rules and boxes.

A page can exist without rules between articles, but sometimes they are needed or can be an important part of the graphic style. White space has the same effect, creating a division between the articles. However, rules can be used in thicker or very thin weights above or below particular text elements, such as bylines. Rules or boxes work well for the folio/header. Solid black or grey boxes can be used for article flags, bylines or pull-quotes. Use boxes, rules or small icon graphics for the page's folio or index.

Dominant Element: the top photo is largest and creates a strong central focal point on the page

2.4.4 PHOTOS/GRAPHICS

Photos or a graphic can improve the design of a page. There should be at least one image per page, and as with the page hierarchy, there should be a dominant photo and successive smaller images, even in the same article. When in doubt, print a good photo as big as possible. Crop tightly and use the horizontal or vertical rectangular shape rather than the static square. When using multiple photos, choose one to be the largest, then vary the size of the remaining images. There is nothing wrong with a large lead photo printed just as large as the article. The photo will be eye-catching because of its size and hopefully its content.

Newspapers should invest in the resources needed for good photojournalism, even if this means just an inexpensive digital camera for grabbing breaking news. Things happen on your campus—shootings, car fires, movie sets, and protests. Keep a disposable film camera in a newsroom desk drawer for those times when you really need to capture the moment. Ask reporters to bring back at least one close-up and one wide shot. Editors should always be thinking of the image to go with a story and designers should be involved in the story meeting, to add their opinion and to be able to suggest how to capture the perfect photo.

Tabloid papers should plan the cover ahead—early in the week and weeks before with special issues. Alternate covers between sections depending on the most important article that issue. Skyboxes and teasers can still be used on the cover, but keep them limited. Your paper is not a supermarket tabloid.

2.4.5 FOLIO / PAGE HEADERS

Each page should have on it basic publication information—the page number otherwise called a folio. Beyond the page number, the folio can include the paper's name, section and date. The folio appears almost near any outside edge of the page and often the folio (just the page number) will appear at the bottom, while a header runs along the top. Each page can also have contact information for the section editor, an index of articles in that section or include photo and graphic credits.

The graphic style of a paper is very much based on the total look of the page, and the folio in combination with the headers forms a great amount of the page's structure. These text elements are very simple and do not need to dominate the page, but they are important bits of information—part branding, part navigation. Indexing the section or at least including the section title navigates the reader through the paper. The page number is likely the most important element in this collection, especially if the cover or table of contents directs readers to a particular page.

2.4.6 MASTHEAD

The masthead—often confused with the nameplate or publication logo (see 2.4.7)—is the list of staff, office location and contact and any additional legal information. Traditionally the masthead appears on an editorial page; however, the element could be placed at the front of a publication with letters or other reader opinion.

2.5 The Whole Page

Once a structure is created for the news page, layout can begin. With each new issue, there are ways to design the page using the structure, but also by using a few design principles and techniques. This section focuses on planning an entire page or even a spread, as one unified design. The individual parts now make up the whole and for the design to be effective, the page must read as one, even when filled with many stories. Designing for the whole page is a set of loose guidelines to make the news look good and serve the reader. This section highlights the design elements, such as white space, color and advertising, which will affect the entire page

2.5.1 USING WHITE SPACE

White space is a utopian dream every designer has, with reason. Bordering an element on the page with empty space attractions attention—or rather put emphasis on the element. Newspapers are beginning to use white space more and more to frame single articles or entire pages. Significant world events may present the need for a broadsheet's cover to suddenly run a small photo floating in a sea of white newsprint. The reader's eye is pulled to the object.

One reason for using a grid with a large number of columns is to allow the text columns to shift over and leave white space to frame the article. That, of course, is speaking vertically, whereas horizontally leaving a gap between two articles is sufficient enough to avoid the use of a rule. Another reason is simply breathing space on a page, especially full-page features that can use the white space as a magazine would, creating an interesting page that doesn't look like a 5 or 6-column news page.

2.5.2 PACKAGED

There are two approaches to packaging articles. The cleanest looking article layout is by far the rectangle—either vertical or horizontal. This may require stacking elements or laying them down side-by-side, but avoid making your layout into a jigsaw puzzle. Packaging, according to Ron Johnson, is used to "serve readers with all related content in the same location." The example on the right illustrates packaging—two related articles have been grouped under one dominant photo and headline, leaving the three article separated by white space. With that amount of white space, a rule is not necessary. As for the shape, all three articles are rectangular—clean, easy to read, easy to layout and simple.

Keeping the article contain in a rectangle will also help structure the page's hierarchy and need not make the page boring. Instead readability is improved which in turn focuses on the importance of the newspaper—the news. Check out any Canadian daily broadsheet—especially ones redesigned in the last five years—for ongoing examples of articles laid out in boxes.

2.5.3 PLACEMENT OF ARTICLE AND OTHER ELEMENTS

Take the page hierarchy a step further and build a structure on the page. If the most important news story takes up three-quarters of the page, leaving a small box at the bottom of the page where the secondary article barely fits, make a choice between jumping part of the lead article or instead taking up the whole

THE STUDENT PRESS | Friday, April 21, 2006 A5

NEWS

Faculty remained on strike for three weeks. Led by a bagpiper, St. James faculty return to classes early Monday morning (below). Dave Kestin photos.

Post-strike semester
Concerns raised after three weeks of missed classes

BY MIKE BARKER | SENIOR NEWS EDITOR

College faculty were paraded back to work ending the three-week strike. Led by a bagpiper the faculty returned to St. James the day before classes resumed.

After last minute negotiations on Friday, March 24, instructors for 24 Ontario colleges agreed to return to the classroom. George Brown College was one of many colleges that decided to resume classes on Tuesday, March 28, while others colleges returned to class the day before.

"We wanted to give [faculty] a day," said Michael Cooke, vice president of academics. "Ideally we would have liked to have given them two or three days, but we felt that that would further penalize the students. At least give the faculty a day to think this through so that when they meet with the students they had a thought through plan."

Faculty returned to classrooms Tuesday to finish the four remaining weeks left this semester. A few programs will continue past the end of the regular semester—Dental Hygiene and Fitness for example—however, most programs will end classes on April 21.

"There are some courses, Dental Hygiene and Fitness, that will actually keep going after April 21, because the students won't have met the outcomes by April 21," said Cooke.

As for the majority of programs faculty have been given room to ensure no student is left behind. One way to give students more time to finish this semester will come from the extension for submitting final marks. Instructors have ten extra days to before marks are due.

"It's also possible within an individual program that if a student needs some more time or some more help just on a personal basis. We try to accommodate that, because our goal is to help each student meet the outcomes," added Cooke.

Class time lost is one concern being raised by students. "I have missed three weeks of classes," said Arlette D'Souza, an international student. "I feel I am completing the semester without the complete course."

For most students, classroom time lost during the strike will not be recouped; instead course material will be condensed. When faculty returned to work, instructors met in consultation with their program chairs to adjust teaching activities to the shorter period.

"The big thing for students is to focus on the outcomes. What are the skills or knowledge that they need at this point in their program," said Cooke.

Cooke further explained "the time and the classes are a means to an end, they're not an end in themselves. Lots of circumstances arise, you're sick, you sleep in, or you have to work. That's not the same as missing the outcomes."

The outcomes can be found in course outlines handed out at the beginning of each semester. These learning goals are based on a wider understanding of the course, rather then specific knowledge.

Due to the three weeks without class, students have been asking about a refunds. On March 31, the Ministry for Training, Colleges and Universities released its' decision regarding a refund.

According to Cooke, "The Ministry is saying that any student, who wishes to withdraw because they feel their success was compromised by the strike, may do so and get a full refund." Further added, "Students hoping for a partial refund will be disappointed with the Ministry's policy"

For a frustrated D'Souza, tuition is not cheap. "I'm a little bit ticked off about the strike because first off, I'm international, I tend to pay around eleven thousand per year and I have to extend my visa if I were to drop this semester and take it again."

"I think there should be a partial refund. In three weeks I've lost a lot of money," said D'Souza. In fact, one week for an international student costs about $367 whereas a domestic student would pay around $80 per week. The total for the three weeks would come out to over $1100 for an international student versus $240 for a domestic student.

When asked about taking some of her concerns to her instructors, D'Souza said, "I think the professors have been pretty concerned about it."

STRIKING FACTS
- 15 days of classes missed
- $2,682 average 3-weeks tuition
- $1100 average 3-weeks tuition for international student
- 9 km: average distance walked on picket line per faculty member

Faculty parade back to work

Led by a bagpiper, a moment of silence was observed Monday by returning faculty in honour of John Stammers, a Centennial instructor who passed away over the weekend from the result of an altercation with a car attempting to cross the picket line.

Toronto Police have already decided not to lay criminal charges on the driver, suggesting that the video surveillance shows Stammers picking a fight with the car. Police hold Stammers responsible for his own actions and refuse to deal with the matter further, inferred a Police spokesperson last week.

"It's a tragedy and my heart goes out to the family of John [Stammers]. He was only a few years from retirement," said George Adelaire, an instructor at the St. James campus. "I think it's ridiculous that the police have suggested John picked the fight with the car. You don't pick a fight with a car—it'll win any day."

The parade ended on King Street with a short speech. Faculty then dispersed to their departments to recover the remaining weeks through the College's semester completion strategy. Faculty were informed of the strategy Monday and given the day to rewrite their courses, dropping some material.

Canadian Collegiate News

Transit fares going up again

BY MIKE BARKER | SENIOR NEWS EDITOR

This was supposed to be the year the TTC dropped fares and metropass prices, but instead fares are going up for the second year in a row at the expense of ridership.

The TTC wanted more funding from city hall, beyond the city council approved 2% maximum increase. With that rejection in hand, facing a short fall from increased fuel costs, added labour expenses, a purchase of new buses and a $10 million fraud ring broken, the TTC was force in a quickly called meeting February 8 to increase fares.

In 2003, The TTC published the Ridership Growth Strategy showing the various strategies for increasing ridership. The report also quantifies the ridership loss with each fare increase.

The strategy is a four step process whereby the TTC starts by meeting "current system needs" identified in 2003, but which has increased because of fuel and labour costs; increase service capacity; implement fare initiatives; and finally expand the Spadina subway north York University and the Sheppard line east to connect with the Scarborough RT.

The extension to York University would cost $1.5 billion dollars and take seven years to build and the Sheppard extension would take nine years at a cost of $2.4 billion—the Sheppard line is currently the most underused subway line.

The TTC has actually implemented initiatives from the third step but these did not take the form of fare and metropass reductions, instead new passes were introduced: the weekly pass and making the monthly pass transferrable. City hall and the TTC have taken much credit for the transferrable pass—which can only be used by one person at a time—yet the $5 decrease initiative did not go through.

For most people TTC improvements are not measurable. Recognizing a streetcar line's frequency has improved goes unnoticed compared to a fare decrease that is a personal reward for each rider—and according to Rocket Rider's transit users group, streetcar lines have not seen improvements.

Ridership levels have not returned to their 1988 peak of 463 million rides that year. While the population of Toronto grew, ridership continued to slide until 1997. It's been climbing back slowly every since, but increases cause set backs—as do labour stoppages.

Blaming the TTC for their lack of funding would be like complaining to Tim Horton's that Starbuck's line up is too slow—talking to the wrong company. The provincial government can be blamed for pulling back on funding levels since the late 1980s. Back then the province paid for half of the operating expenses and three-quarters of capital expenses and until last year the province kicked in nothing. However, the TTC has been blamed for improvements few riders want—replacing buses doesn't add more buses to the fleet. As for the streetcars, new ones are at least five years away.

There is also an expectation that the federal government will kick in some money to transit. Since they haven't now or at all, that should not be an expectation. Previously in Ontario the province helped transit and

page. Rather than lay out a tight news page with the photo squeezed into three columns, let the article dominate the entire page. Read the sub-section below for the grander hierarchy beyond one page.

2.5.4 SINGLE PAGE VS. SPREAD

Often layout and design thinking for the news is on a page-by-page basis. There is a place for this method, but when the reader pulls open the paper the entire spread is viewed. When approaching the design of a paper, attempt to keep the pages together as spreads, starting with the template in spreads. Even though most newspapers are not saddle-stitched and the pages will shift and fall away, nothing is stopping the layout from stretching across the spread. Run a photo large, split between the two pages, aligning dead space in the image over the spine. Wrap the article around this.

2.5.6 INTEGRATING ADVERTISING

A trend in newspaper layout among free papers—the alt-weeklies—is to fill an entire page with ads and keep them separate from the editorial content. This is a mistake unless your paper gets enough ads that cover over 70 per cent of the total page real estate. Advertising helps fund the newspaper and the ads deserve to be spread throughout the paper. If clustered, those ad pages overwhelm the reader. The average newspaper reader is already comfortable with ads spread through out a publication.

Be flexible with ad placement and allow for variation in ad size. There will be tall, skinny ads that have to be placed along the length of the page—the general rule is to place these on the outside edge of a spread. Wide, short ads, including quarter page ads, can be placed side-by-side aligned to the bottom of the page. Leave the news to the top. The key is to place ads in a rectangular formation and should any space appear, use these gaps for public service announcements or house ads.

Every once in a while an ad will come along that takes up all-but-one-column in width and two-thirds to three-quarters of the page vertically. Advertisers may be doing a large national or regional

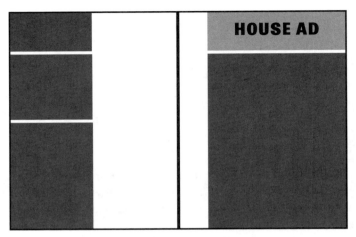

Outside edge stacked   All-but-one-column

campaign and one size was chosen that fit best in many papers, or the advertiser might be maximizing the page without buying a full page. This size of ad creates a challenge for the designer. If an article can't be wrapped around the ad and there are no ads to fill some of the gaps, create a house ad to sit on top of the paid ad and run a one column article or text jumped from another page.

For page with many ads of varying sizes, use the larger ads on bottom and smaller on top. The weight of the large ads should sit at the bottom, rather than weigh down the top of the page.

2.5.7 SKYBOXES, TEASERS, NEWS BITES AND WINDOWS

There are many ways to approach laying out small snippets of information and teasers to other sections. Skyboxes usually refer to the visual teasers around the nameplate on the cover page, however, designing a skybox bar across an inside bar—or even along the bottom—may be a good place to leave short bits of news such as quotes, teasers to other sections, upcoming events. The National Post designed a similar information bar when it launched, often using the space for columnists.

Another option is to have a running table of contents bar for each section highlighting the current article and alluding to the following pages.

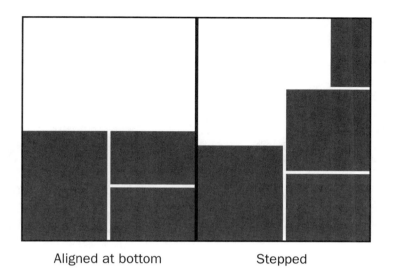

Aligned at bottom   Stepped

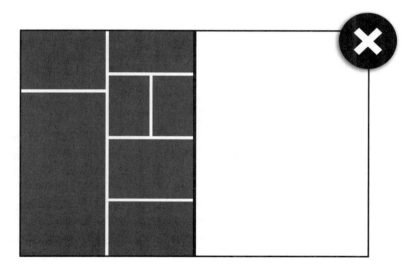

Avoid filling one page: while this layout option will create a full empty editorial page, the ad page is cluttered and poor ad placement practice.

2.6 Template and Style Guide

This sub-section focused on the creation of a template for repeat use with each successive issue and a visual representation on paper that shows the visual identity system in its entirety.

Using a template system can be very involved or simple. In this case, the template is a layout software document that is usually blank and ready for fresh copy. A template can consist of one two-page spread that is set with all the paper's sections ready to go, or a series of files for each section and type of page—even one template file that allows for blocking in specific advertising space. The best reason for having a simple yet flexible template is to make the designer more efficient. Newspapers have tight deadlines and short production periods whether publishing daily, weekly or bi-weekly.

Another system for improving efficiency is in having a Library containing copies of each repeating graphical element, even the linked text boxes for varying column articles.

To leave a lasting memory or in order to create a visual reminder of the paper's visual identity, a style guide can also be created. The sophistication can vary from a simple poster displaying a sample page with annotated notes for each element or an entire booklet outlining the entire process and every element down to the smallest detail.

2.6.1 GRID

This design process began with the grid. Now the grid will be revisited to lock it into the final design. Begin with a fresh layout document set to the proper page size and allowing for the borders to create the image area necessary. Set up the columns in the master page plus all necessary guidelines for the structure or modules. The grid is necessary to keep those performing layout working within the visual identity.

2.6.2 SETTING THE STYLE-SHEETS

Quark and InDesign both allow for text style settings to be saved and applied to unstyled selections of text. Keyboard shortcuts can also be applied to the styles, which speeds up layout and makes the designer more efficient.

INDESIGN:

There are two types of text styles for InDesign: **Paragraph** and **Character Styles**. When assigning a text style in the Paragraph palette, the style will be applied to all lines of text selected between paragraph returns (also known as carriage returns). Placing the cursor between letters on one line and then applying a Paragraph style will only take effect forward and back to the nearest Paragraph mark. These are especially useful for applying the main styles to each line as needed and even selecting all the body text then in one click or keystroke applying the appropriate style.

The Character Styles only effect individual characters highlighted and then applied with a Character Style. The styles are useful for formatting text—applying the drop cap or paragraph embedded formatting, such as italics. Versions of InDesign since the Creative Suite (CS) edition have Nested Styles that will automatically apply the drop cap style and a series of nested styles between specific hidden characters such as a tab.

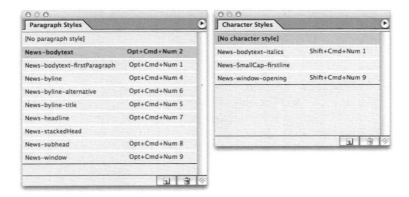

InDesign: the Paragraph and Character Styles palettes can contain the newspaper's text styles. Using the Styles will make layout quicker and easier, while helping maintain the consistent use of typography throughout. InDesign also allows keyboard short-cuts to speed up production even more — only the number pad keys 1 to 10 work.

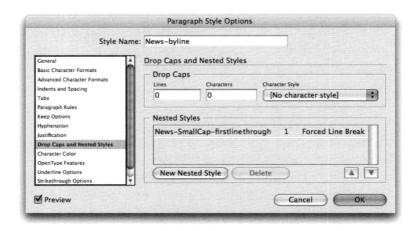

Nested styles: settings under paragraph style options which allow character styles to be embedded automatically in a block of text.

Rice releases
Best-selling author creates a

BY MIKE BARKER
Arts&Culture Editor

CHRISTOPHER RICE, A 26-YEAR-OLD AMERICAN author who has already penned two New York Times bestsellers, has hit the road to promote his newest book, *Light Before Day*.

As with Rice's two previous books, *Density of Soul* and *The Snow Garden*, *Light Before Day*

While Adam str
—drinking binge
ing to terms wit
alcoholic mothe
the disappearan
the dark world
Hollywood's gay
in California's ce
For Rice, writ

Nested style example: here the paragraph is set in lino letter small caps up to a soft return (shift-return), then the text is set in lino letter roman for the remainder.

QUARK:

Quark Xpress also has a style palette for paragraph and character styles. From the **Edit** menu, choose **Style Sheets...** to open the editing window.

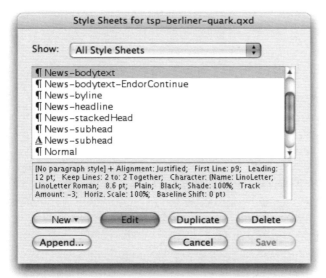

Quark style sheets: type can be styled by clicking the style in the Style Sheets palette (top). Style Sheets are edited in the Style Sheet window.

2.6.3 LIBRARY

A Library file is a great way of keeping track of repeating graphical and text elements that appear in the newspaper. The file can also contain house ads and repeating photographs such as columnist headshots. The normal method for using a Library is to design the element, then import in into the Library file (by dragging the group or selected grouping).

2.6.4 STYLE GUIDE

The simplest way to make a style guide is to take an existing layout or the template filled in, then export one or more pages as in PDF or EPS format. Place this graphic in a fresh layout document and create the notes around it that will annotate each element. Many papers have laser printers with tabloid printing, and for those that don't, lay out the style guide on several letter-sized page and crop the exported page to the portions you need to annotate. Another simple method would be to post a page from the newspaper on a wall and attach printed labels of each element.

Large, busy papers may need to create a full booklet with every element carefully labeled and dissected to which design staff can refer. The reason for any of these options is to ensure that future staff will be able to continue the current design and if there becomes a need to redesign, be able to understand how the previous one happened. In many ways, a good redesign might last many years over a great amount of turnover.

Folio (section and page no.)

Franklin Gothic Demi
18pt, 80% black, Flush left

Section header

Franklin Gothic Medium
30pt, 100% black
ALL CAPS, Flush left

Headline w/subhead

Lino Letter Bold
32pt plus, Flush left

Subhead

Franklin Gothic Medium Cond.
Point size half of headline
70% black, Flush left

Byline

Lino Letter
Name: Bold Small Caps
Title: Medium Small Caps
Spacer: | (pipe)
8.6/12pt, Flush left
Style:
A:
BY NAME | POSITION

B:
BY NAME
POSITION TOO LONG OR WIRE TITLE

Body text

Lino Letter Roman
8.6/12pt, Justified,
Baseline grid align
9pt first line indent
Drop Cap:
3-line, not indent
Lino Letter Bold

Baseline grid

12pt grid for aligning text
and using for spacing

A8

NEWS

Students and

Concerns raised after three wee

BY MIKE BARKER | SENIOR REPORTER

College faculty paraded back to work ending the three-week strike. Led by a bagpiper the faculty returned to St. James the day before classes resumed.

After last minute negotiations on Friday, March 24, instructors for 24 Ontario colleges agreed to return to the classroom. George Brown College was one of many colleges that decided to resume classes on Tuesday, March 28, while others colleges returned to class the day before.

"We wanted to give [faculty] a day," said Michael Cooke, vice president of academics. "Ideally we would have liked to have given them two or three days, but we felt that that would further penalize the students. At least give the faculty a day to think this through so that when they meet with the students they had a thought through plan."

Faculty returned to classrooms Tuesday to finish the four remaining weeks left this semester. A few programs will continue past the end of the regular semester—Dental Hygiene and Fitness for example—however most pro-

STRIKING FACTS
- 15 days of classes missed
- $240: average 3-weeks tuition
- $1100: average 3-weeks tuition for international student
- 9 km: average distance walked on picket line per faculty member

"There are some co Hygiene and Fitness, th ly keep going after Apr the students won't have comes by April 21," said

As for the majority faculty have been given sure no student is left way to give students mo ish this semester will c extension for submittin Instructors have ten ext fore marks are due.

"It's also po an individual if a student more time o help just on a sis. We try to that, because help each stu outcomes," ad Class time concern bein students. "I three weeks said Arlette D ternational st am completin ter without the complet

For most students time lost during the st be recouped; instead ri will be condensed. returned to work ins

Column grid

20 columns across
(set text in multiples of 4 or 5)

Info box

Franklin Gothic Book Cond.
9 /10.8pt, Flush left
White on 70% black or 100% spot
1 pica text wrap spacer around

2.7 Using Color

Color usage has been divided into two parts for this book. For a technical approach to managing colors in layout and production, refer to the Production step of this book. As for using color as an element of design, begin with what you have for each page. Most small papers do not have the financial resources to print color on every page, and the printer for large and small papers might not be able to put full color down on every page. Reproduction quality is also an issue for all newspapers. As printing presses improve, the color quality rises and more colorful daily papers hit the stands. Unless your paper is printed on the same press as your local daily and to the exact same standards, don't expect to get the same color quality in your paper.

As the designer, it is good to know the limits of your paper and the press the paper is printed on. Most newspapers use the grey sponge-like material called newsprint. Oftentimes printing black yields dark grey instead. Spot colors have more chance of surviving because your printer will match a specific color—make sure your paper has a Pantone swatch book for reference and don't trust the colors on the monitor. "Use spot color only as punctuation", says Ron Johnson. Spot colors work best in small amounts where they are more noticeable because of their minimal presence on the page.

Printing CMYK—full color made from 4 plate printing with Cyan, Magenta, Yellow and blacK—will vary depending on the pressman's view of what looks right and balancing the colors on each spread. Simply put, a color from a CMYK swatch book is less likely to match on newsprint. Try printing various combinations of colors you would like to use and see which turn out best.

At the beginning of each year or with new staff taking over design and production, it makes very good sense to visit your printer. The printer is very knowledgeable about the press machines and can inform you on color placement, imposition and paper stock. Ask your printer how long it takes to run your paper through the press—this information might surprise you. Finally, get from your printer their imposition charts (also called pagination charts) to assist you on knowing where color goes. Further explanation on imposition can also be found in the Production section.

Depending on your paper's size and your printer, printing the cover in full-color also means you have color on the centre spread and the back cover—hopefully the back cover is an ad or several ads that paid for the color in the first place.

On pages where an advertiser has paid for full-color or a spot color, be conservative in your use of the color. This is especially true where the spot color is that company's choice for their official spot color and is meant to draw attention to their ad, rather than your layout. Further tips on ad placement can be found later in this section.

More than just black: a tint of black can add color to the page and helps break up a stark black and white only page. Use a tint for some text or graphic elements to vary the amount of black on the page. Text over color, including a tint, can make the type hard to read. The higher the contrast, the more readable the type, such as white on 80 to 100 per cent black.

2.7.1 THE RIGHT COLOR

Approaching color usage should be consistent with the overall design and use of type. The trend is to change the color used on the cover every issue, especially with a magazine style tabloid. On front pages where news runs, leave the color to the nameplate, skyboxes, photos and ads. Your paper's nameplate is its brand and should remain consistent as well—choose or find the color that represents your paper, such as the color of your news boxes or stands. The same consistency should exist inside your paper—if the news section always has color, then use the same color every issue for the graphic elements.

The rainbow is a wonderful collection of colors, but never should all be used together. There are some collections of color that don't work together even if a part of a brand—take the Olympic rings for example, which have five colors that don't play nice together, but work well in Olympic branding or in the daily newspaper because of the minimal usage. When finding a palette of colors, stick to a maximum of four.

Also color appeals to individual tastes. There is a system of color reproduction, Pantone, that designers and printers use to agree on what blue looks like—or a hundred variations of blue. Having a Pantone swatch book is a good idea for a newspaper. At the very least, purchase an inexpensive color sourcebook.

There are several ways color is printed and many swatch books. In a perfect world your paper could afford the complete set; otherwise, choose between the Pantone Solid uncoated and Pantone Process. Process shows many of the Pantone solid colors made from CMYK and the Solid book has the solid inks of the Pantone swatch system. Because newsprint is uncoated paper, you will be using the uncoated version of a Pantone color, though there is little variation between coated and uncoated. Also remember that newsprint is not normally white paper and presses vary in their application of color, which will in turn affect the accuracy of your color.

2.7.2. WHEN TO VARY THE COLORS

Once a consistent visual identity has been established, begin breaking the mold with one section, preferably the feature article. Where full color falls inside the paper is a good place to experiment with layout and (see THE NEXT STEP). In these cases use the color that fits the article—a recycling story on blue and green bins may point to blue and green for the colors; a fashion feature may have great photos with colors and can be pulled into the design.

2.7.3 GRAPHIC ELEMENTS AND COLOR

As mentioned before, even a shade of black on the byline varies the elements on the page. The same can be said for non-text elements such as rules, boxes and graphics. Vary the color of boxes and rules with shades of gray and punctuate with color when it seems appropriate. Be careful, as large blocks of color will cause a distraction away from the news.

Cyan, Magenta, Yellow and Black: these four inks are combined to produce full-colour printed material. High-end printing will often use additional inks for greater colour variation and effect, but this is unlikely in a newspaper.

Spot colour: like punctuation, spot colour use is sparse, yet effective.

2.8 The Next Step

There are a number of ways to take news design to the next level. An efficient designer will have more time to focus on visually communicating the written words and there are a few visual additions that can be added to news design.

2.8.1 LAYOUT TIPS/TRICKS

Working efficiently as a designer is about working smartly and saving seconds that can translate into many hours. Keyboard shortcuts, style-sheet shortcuts and libraries are simple ways to speed up repetitive work. Working smartly prevents all-night work and is time saved that can be focused on better design.

The next layer of shortcuts is directly related to layout. How layout is done can help speed up laying out the page. In the template subsection the Library was discussed as a place to save basic article text boxes.

When approaching the page, take a second to plan out the layout—know how many words fit on a page, how many articles need to go on a page and which one is most important. Knowing this can help prevent shuffling articles around later. As well, being aware of the placement, importance and length can mean knowing to grab the 5-column article in the Library.

Keep text boxes linked and flow the text from box to box, using each box for a particular element—the headline and sub-headline box linked to one 5-column text box. Using just one text box with columns can greatly help layout when needing to adjust the length and placement.

2.8.2 LAYOUT WITH MEANING

Typography, imagery and layout can have a great effect on telling the story visually. This happens most often with features, but there is no reason the same principle can't be applied to news or sports articles. Especially with the use of photography, a news article can be brought to life. A news piece covering the state of on-campus cafeteria food would work will with images from the cafeteria: students eating, paying for food and moving quickly off

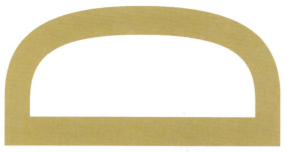

Giving meaning to layout: type can be used to illustrate articles, starting with the headline. This type hamburger pairs well with a related article.

to class. Several images of varying size can portray a sense of a fast moving and crowded environment.

A number of designers prefer to use the typography as expressive illustrations related to the article. An article highlighting a recent study on fast food consumption could turn the headline into a hamburger.

2.8.3   INFORMATION GRAPHICS

The use of information graphics to tell a story is very popular among mainstream newspapers. Graphics go beyond the obvious statistical information to explain a series of events or a process. A writer can very easily explain in words the same idea, so why would a paper run information graphics instead? The goal should be to make the reader understand the information almost on first glance. As well, graphics liven up the page and add a layer of storytelling to the news.

Info-graphics: above, a fictional accident is retold through an info graphic when no photos were available. The graphic below compares voter turnout in three recent elections—the percentage is represented by how much each ballot box is filled.

2004 Federal Election
Voter turnout 60.9%[1]

2003 Ontario Election
Voter turnout 56.9%[2]

2003 Québec Election
Voter turnout 70.42%[3]

Applications for information graphics in the news are numerous. Sports coverage can recount plays or team statistics using innovative graphics—the icon of a hockey puck to express wins or using the center line on the ring for positive or negative comparisons to other teams in the region; news coverage can use piles of cash increasing with tuition or show the number of students current tuition costs would pay for in the 60s and just as the big papers do, use the graphics to explain the share of the vote by slate for your local or student government.

Information graphics don't have to replace the news and can work in tandem. When struggling to find a graphic for a story on the lack of recycling in your community, have the designer experiment with a simple stat from the article. Bar, pie, line graphs are all ways of expressing stats graphically, but they can be a bit dull. Apply a metaphor or symbol to represent the data collected.

Throughout this book there have been a number of information illustrations that have explained concepts as a series of steps. Try using the idea applied to any how-to—how to use a U-pass, how to park on campus; how to line up properly at the coffee shop or how to ride a bus and move to the back when it's filling.

2.8.4   INNOVATION IN NEWS DESIGN

The Internet is changing the way news is delivered just as the television affected news delivery decades ago. And while television news did not kill this antiquated beast, the Internet is causing the newspaper to adapt. Television revolutionized the speed of breaking news, but lacks the diversity and deeper coverage newspapers provide. Now the Internet is instant and offers unlimited space for broad news coverage. Technology forces changes in other ways for newspapers. North American presses are shrinking, which makes the broadsheets skinnier and the tabs squatter. Readers expect easy-to-hold papers yet the established broadsheets refuse to reformat as tabloids for fear of losing respect.

While the Internet is offering a place for lengthy analysis that was once the domain of the newspaper, reading long passages on screen becomes a strain on the eyes. Newspapers should continue the lengthy analysis and invent a new paradigm of news coverage. Just as journalism will adapt, design in the paper will as well.

2.8.5   NEW IDEAS

The following pages show a variety of design styles with the same set of articles. The examples range from sophisticated to radical.

A2 • NEWS   Saturday, December 23, 2006 | THE STUDENT PRESS

FACULTY STRIKE '06

Faculty returned from the three-week long strike Monday, led by a bagpiper. A moment of silence was observed for fellow instructor John Stammers, who passed away Saturday. Mike Barker photo

Students and faculty resume semester
Concerns raised after three weeks of missed classes

BY MIKE BARKER
SENIOR REPORTER

College faculty paraded back to work ending the three-week strike. Led by a bagpiper the faculty returned to St. James the day before classes resumed.

After last minute negotiations on Friday, March 24, instructors for 24 Ontario colleges agreed to return to the classroom. George Brown College was one of many colleges that decided to resume classes on Tuesday, March 28, while others colleges returned to class the day before.

"We wanted to give [faculty] a day," said Michael Cooke, vice president of academics. "Ideally we would have liked to have given them two or three days, but we felt that what would further penalize the students. At least give the faculty a day to think this through so that when they meet with the students they had a thought through plan."

Faculty returned to classrooms Tuesday to finish the four remaining weeks left this semester. A few programs will continue past the end of the regular semester—Dental Hygiene and Fitness for example—however, most programs will end classes on April 21.

"There are some courses, Dental Hygiene and Fitness, that will actually keep going after April 21, because the students won't have met the outcomes by April 21," said Cooke.

As for the majority of programs faculty have been given room to ensure no student is left behind. One way to give students more time to finish this semester will come from the extension for submitting final marks. Instructors have ten extra days to before marks are due.

"It's also possible within an individual program that if a student needs some more time or some more help just on a personal basis. We try to accommodate that, because our goal is to help each student meet the outcomes," added Cooke.

Class time lost is one concern being raised by students. "I have missed three weeks of classes," said Arlette D'Souza, an international student. "I feel I am completing the semester without the complete course."

For most students, classroom time lost during the strike will not be recouped, instead course material will be condensed. When faculty returned to work, instructors met in consultation with their program chairs to adjust teaching activities to the shorter period.

"The big thing for students is to focus on the outcomes. What are the skills or knowledge that they need at this point in their program," said Cooke.

Cooke further explained "the time and the classes are a means to an end, they're not an end in themselves. Lots of circumstances arise, you're sick, you sleep in, or you have to work. That's not the same as missing the outcomes."

The outcomes can be found in all course outlines handed out at the beginning of each semester by instructors. These learning goals are based on a wider understanding of the course, rather then specific knowledge.

Due to the three weeks without class, students have been asking about a refunds. On March 31, the Ministry for Training, Colleges and Universities released its' decision regarding a refund.

According to Cooke, "The Ministry is saying that any student, who wishes to withdraw because they feel that their success was compromised by the strike, may do so and get a full refund. He further added, "Students hoping for a partial refund will be disappointed with the Ministry's policy."

For a frustrated D'Souza, tuition is not cheap. "I'm a little bit ticked off about the strike because first off, I'm international, I tend to pay around eleven thousand per year and I have to extend my visa if I were to drop this semester and take it again."

STRIKING FACTS

15
Days of school missed

$240
3-weeks tuition (average)

$1100
3-weeks tuition (average) for International student

9km
Average distanced walked on the picket line

Return to classes marked by tragedy

BY GEORGE BROWN | EDUCATION BEAT

A moment of silence was observed Monday by returning faculty in honour of John Stammers, a Centennial instructor who passed away over the weekend from the result of an altercation with a car attempting to cross the picket line.

Toronto Police have already decided not to lay criminal charges on the driver, suggesting that the video survilence shows Stammers picking a fight with the car.

Police hold Stammers responsible for his own actions and refuse to deal with the matter further, inferred a Police spokesperson last week.

"It's a tragedy and my heart goes out to the family of John [Stammers]. He was only a few years from retirement," said George Adelaide, an instructor at the St. James campus. "I think it's rediculous that the police have suggested John picked the fight with the car. You don't pick a fight with a car—it'll win any day."

While instructors returned to St. James, a bagpiper led a moment of silence and a pressesion through the three campus building. Students, college staff and security looked on in confusion as the bagpiper mounted through the halls, passed the lone Tim Horton's.

Due to the three weeks without class, students have been asking about a refunds. On March 31, the Ministry for Training, Colleges and Universities released its' decision regarding a refund.

"It's a tragedy and my heart goes out to the family of John [Stammers]. He was only a few years from retirement," said George Adelaide, an instructor at the St. James campus. "I think it's rediculous that the police have suggested John picked the fight with the car. You don't pick a fight with a car—it'll win any day."

While instructors returned to St. James, a bagpiper led a moment of silence and a pressesion through the three campus building. Students, college staff and security looked on in confusion as the bagpiper mounted through the halls, even through business and finance.

Sophisticated: a news page with color. A dominant photo sits near the top, color is used in the photo and as punctuation, emphasizing the page's topic and the sidebar. This design uses Lino Letter and ITC Franklin Gothic, using the serif typography in a classic way and the sans serif as contrasting element.

THE STUDENT PRESS | Saturday, December 23, 2006

ARTS • A3

CULTURE

Twelve channels on the dial was enough
Retro Canadian television and the one channel universe

BY MIKE BARKER | ARTS&CULTURE

Imagine turning on your television today to find that you only have one channel to watch and for some reason, it's in black and white. Not so long ago Canadian viewers had very few channels to watch—three in most cities—and cable was not yet popular, as it offered no better choice.

The first Canadian television broadcast began with a news item hosted by Lorne Green—before he left Canada to star in the American western drama Bonanza. Television in Canada started in 1952 with one network broadcasting in English and French, the Canadian Broadcasting Corporation (CBC)/ Société Radio-Canada (SRC). Only Canadians in Toronto and Montreal could watch CBC the first year, but by 1955 the CBC/Radio-Canada had expanded to reach 66 per cent of the Canadian population.

The CBC/Radio-Canada enjoyed nine years dominating the Canadian airwaves, although there had always been American broadcast signals sneaking across the border. In 1961, the CTV Network began broadcasting, with the permission of the CBC—which meant they created their own competition. The CBC controlled broadcasting in Canada until the Canadian Radio-Television Commission (CRTC) was established in 1968.

In the early days of the CRTC, the rules governing Canadian television were established, including granting licenses and controlling amounts of Canadian content. 1970 brought the first content regulations making sure that all TV broadcasters in Canada had to fill their schedules with at least 60 per cent Canadian content.

Television grew slightly in the 1970s with the first private French-language network,

TVA in 1971 and Global in 1974—as well as educational channels TV Ontario, Access Alberta and B.C.'s Knowledge network. In 1972, Toronto saw the launch of City-TV, which has served as the base for many more channels.

Moses Znaimer, considered a guru of Canadian television, started at the CBC as an interviewer for the program Take 30 (with former Governor General Adrianne Clarkson). Moses helped give birth to City and it's many offspring. When City started broadcasting, it was from the former Electric Circus Nightclub on Queen East.

The explosion on cable did not begin until the mid-1980s when the CRTC allowed pay-TV and speciality channels to open. Canadians finally had more choice as CBC Newsworld, YTV, Vision TV, Muchmusic, pay TV channel Family Channel and many more were all broadcasting by 1987. Since the 80s Canadian cable had grown into the hundreds of channels.

The Programs

Any look at retro decades needs a look at Canadian television over the last 50 years. Speciality networks rerun Canadian classics that many Canadians grew up with. Remember Danger Bay, The Odyssey, Polka Dot Door, Today's Special, The Racoons, Fraggle Rock (yes this Jim Henson Muppet classic was made in Canada), The Forest Rangers, Adventures in Rainbow Country, King of Kensington, Seeing Things, Street Legal, Smith and Smith, Fred Penner's Place, The Elephant Show and the Romper Room, just to name a few Canadian classics?

The CBC has embraced their television history with a "retro line" of t-shirts with past CBC logos—from the early days of colour to the evolving familiar logo of today.

Currently, a number of items from CBC's children's programming are on display at the CBC Museum at the CBC Broadcast Centre in Toronto. Mr. Dressup's Tickle-trunk and drawing easel and the set from The Friendly Giant can be seen there.

Sitting in CBC's Museum are a few icons of Canadian television, a trunk and a few puppets. These simple items entertained and delighted several generations of children in English Canada.

There are many unique shows that were produced in Canada over the past fifty years. Here are just a few not mentioned above that were aimed mostly at viewers under 20.

The Friendly Giant

Over 3000 15-minute episodes were produced between 1958 and 1985 featuring the massive Friendly Giant, played by Bob Homme. Friendly would welcome children at the beginning of each show and then let them into his castle through the drawbridge. Once inside, you were invited to "look up, look w-a-a-a-y up" as the camera panned up to Friendly standing by a window with Jerome the Giraffe and Rusty the Rooster. For over 30 years, Friendly's patient smile welcomed children to enjoy stories, music and humour each weekday morning on CBC.

Mr. Dressup

Before we had the Tickle-trunk, there was Butternut Square, a show that after 3 years on air led to Mr. Dressup in 1967. Until 1996, the show aired weekday mornings from Toronto with the familiar Mr. Dressup (Ernie Coombs), and two puppets from Butternut Square: Casey, a 4-year old boy and Finnegan (both of whom left in 1990 with their puppeteer Judith Lawrence).

Coombs came to Canada with his friend Fred Rogers and stayed when Rogers returned to his new American show, Mr. Rogers Neighbourhood. Before leaving, Rogers took a few ideas with him, including the trolley, developed by CBC.

Each day Mr. Dressup would open his Tickle-trunk and pull out a new costume, which he would don for viewers. In 2001, Coombs visited Simon Fraser University in Vancouver to give a "performance" in the campus pub—a chance to record Coombs live with an adult audience for the CBC program Life and Times. That evening filled the pub with over 300 adult fans whom had grown up on Mr. Dressup.

Degrassi

This teen classic recently entered its 25th year, though it has not been on the air for this entire time. A new generation is growing up on the current group in this realistic teen drama, and like the generation before them, these teens tackle the real life events teens battle everyday: drug use, alcoholism, peer-pressure, popularity, AIDS, homophobia, gun violence and suicide. Yeah, that's what my high school was like.

The Edison Twins

This show was based on a brother-sister team made up of Tom and Annie Edison, two teenaged twins who used science to solve mysteries without being overly educational. Each show ended with an explanation of the experiment in that episode that solved the case—and the lesson was still entertaining. Corey Haim got his start on the Edison Twins and over its six season run on the CBC, the twins' parents were played by two different sets of actor—but then again, the parents were hardly ever involved in the story lines.

Childhood memories from the CBC Museum at the CBC Broadcast centre, Mr. Dressup's drawing table, Tickle-trunk, Casey's treehouse, Friendly's guest seating and castle.

Sophisticated: this arts page groups the text as a contained rectangular box with the photos grouped as a single block using the grid to use varing sizes of images. A single dominant image remains in this design. The folio runs the width of the page, creating navigation and information organization.

page 8
news
Saturday/December 23/06

Faculty returned from the three-week long strike Monday, led by a bagpiper. A moment of silence was observed for fellow instructor John Stammers, who passed away Saturday. Mike Barker photo.

Students and faculty resume semester
Concerns raised after three weeks of missed classes

by mike barker
senior reporter

College faculty paraded back to work ending the three-week strike. Led by a bagpiper the faculty returned to St. James the day before classes resumed.

After last minute negotiations on Friday, March 24, instructors for 24 Ontario colleges agreed to return to the classroom. George Brown College was one of many colleges that decided to resume classes on Tuesday, March 28, while others colleges returned to class the day before.

"We wanted to give [faculty] a day," said Michael Cooke, vice president of academics. "Ideally we would have liked to have given them two or three days, but we felt that that would further penalize the students. At least give the faculty a day to think this through so that when they meet with the students they had a thought through plan."

Faculty returned to classrooms Tuesday to finish the four remaining weeks left this semester. A few programs will continue past the end of the regular semester—Dental Hygiene and Fitness for example—however, most programs will end classes on April 21.

"There are some courses, Dental Hygiene and Fitness, that will actually keep going after April 21, because the students won't have met the outcomes by April 21," said Cooke.

As for the majority of programs faculty have been given room to ensure no student is left behind. One way to give students more time to finish this semester will come from the extension for submitting final marks. Instructors have ten extra days to before marks are due.

"It's also possible within an individual program that if a student needs some more time or some more help just on a personal basis. We try to accommodate that, because our goal is to help each student meet the outcomes," added Cooke.

Class time lost is one concern being raised by students. "I have missed three weeks of classes," said Arlette D'Souza, an international student. "I feel I am completing the semester without the complete course."

For most students, classroom time lost during the strike will not be recouped; instead course material will be condensed. When faculty returned to work, instructors met in consultation with their program chairs to adjust teaching activities to the shorter period.

"The big thing for students is to focus on the outcomes. What are the skills or knowledge that they need at this point in their program," said Cooke.

Cooke further explained "the time and the classes are a means to an end, they're not an end in themselves. Lots of circumstances arise, you're sick, you sleep in, or you have to work. That's not the same as missing the outcomes."

The outcomes can be found in all course outlines handed out at the beginning of each semester by instructors. These learning goals are based on a wider understanding of the course, rather then specific knowledge.

Due to the three weeks without class, students have been asking about a refunds. On March 31, the Ministry for Training, Colleges and Universities released its' decision regarding a refund.

According to Cooke, "The Ministry is saying that any student, who wishes to withdraw because they feel that their success was compromised by the strike, may do so and get a full refund. He further added, "Students hoping for a partial refund will be disappointed with the Ministry's policy."

For a frustrated D'Souza, tuition is not cheap. "I'm a little bit ticked off about the strike because first off, I'm international. I tend to pay around eleven thousand per year and I have to extend my visa if I were to drop this semester and take it again."

"I think there should be a partial refund. In three weeks I've lost a lot of money," added D'Souza. In fact, one week for an international student costs about $367 whereas a domestic student would pay around $80 per week.

When asked about taking some of her concerns to her instructors, D'Souza said, "I think the professors have been pretty concerned about it."

"I took my own concerns to one of my professors and I said if I fail this course I cannot graduate and I don't get to search for a job. And my professor said, 'I've received your projects; I'm going to grade you on them. Don't worry about it. I'm going to make sure you get the grade.'" said D'Souza further.

STRIKING FACTS

15 Days of school missed

9km Average distance walked per faculty member

$240 3-weeks tuition (average)

$1100 3-weeks tuition (average) for International student

Bold and artsy: the two sample layouts above and right feature heavy use of Helvetica. While a popular and overused typeface. Helvetica can look good if used properly by using size and a variety of weights to achieve contrast. The folio on this design creates bold, in-your-face navigation.

page 9

arts&culture

Saturday/December 23/06

Twelve channels on the dial was enough

Retro Canadian television and the one channel universe

by mike barker
arts&culture

Childhood memories from the CBC Museum at the CBC Broadcast centre, Tickle-trunk (above) to Friendly's castle (below)

Imagine turning on your television today to find that you only have one channel to watch and for some reason, it's in black and white. Not so long ago Canadian viewers had very few channels to watch—three in most cities—and cable was not yet popular; as it offered no better choice.

The first Canadian television broadcast began with a news item hosted by Lorne Green—before he left Canada to star in the American western drama Bonanza. Television in Canada started in 1952 with one network broadcasting in English and French, the Canadian Broadcasting Corporation (CBC)/Société Radio-Canada (SRC). Only Canadians in Toronto and Montreal could watch CBC the first year, but by 1955 the CBC/Radio-Canada had expanded to reach 66 per cent of the Canadian population.

The CBC/Radio-Canada enjoyed nine years dominating the Canadian airwaves, although there had always been American broadcast signals sneaking across the border. In 1961, the CTV Network began broadcasting, with the permission of the CBC—which meant they created their own competition. The CBC controlled broadcasting in Canada until the Canadian Radio and Television Commission (CRTC) was established in 1968.

In the early days of the CRTC, the rules governing Canadian television were established, granting licenses and controlling amounts of Canadian content. 1970 brought the first content regulations making sure that all TV broadcasters in Canada had to fill their schedules with at least 60 per cent Canadian content.

Television grew slightly in the 1970s with the first private French-language network, TVA in 1971 and Global in 1974—as well as educational channels TV Ontario, Access Alberta and B.C.'s Knowledge network. In 1972, Toronto saw the launch of City-TV, which has served as the base for many more channels.

Moses Znaimer, considered a guru of Canadian television, started at the CBC as an interviewer for the program Take 30 (with former Governor General Adrianne Clarkson). Moses helped give birth to City and it's many offspring. When City started broadcasting, it was from the former Electric Circus Nightclub on Queen East.

The explosion on cable did not begin until the mid-1980s when the CRTC allowed pay-TV and speciality channels to open. Canadians finally had more choice as CBC Newsworld, YTV, Vision TV, Muchmusic, pay TV channel Family Channel and many more were all broadcasting by 1987. Since the 80s Canadian cable had grown into the hundreds of channels.

The Friendly Giant

Over 3000 15-minute episodes were produced between 1958 and 1985 featuring the massive Friendly Giant, played by Bob Homme. Friendly would welcome children at the beginning of each show and then let them into his castle through the drawbridge. Once inside, you were invited to "look up, look w-a-a-a-y up" as the camera panned up to Friendly standing by a window with Jerome the Giraffe and Rusty the Rooster. For over 30 years, Friendly's patient smile welcomed children to enjoy stories, music and humour each weekday morning on CBC.

Mr. Dressup

Before we had the Tickle-trunk, there was Butternut Square, a show that after 3 years on air led to Mr. Dressup in 1967. Until 1996, the show aired weekday mornings from Toronto with the familiar Mr. Dressup (Ernie Coombs), and two puppets from Butternut Square: Casey, a 4-year old boy and Finnegan (both of whom left in 1990 with their puppeteer Judith Lawrence).

Coombs came to Canada with his friend Fred Rogers—you know, Mr. Rogers—and stayed when Rogers returned to his new American show, Mr. Rogers Neighbourhood. Before leaving, Rogers took a few ideas with him, including the trolley, developed by CBC.

Each day Mr. Dressup would open his Tickle-trunk and pull out a new costume, which he would don for viewers. In 2001, Coombs visited Simon Fraser University in Vancouver to give a "performance" in the campus pub—a chance to record Coombs live with an adult audience for the CBC program Life and Times. That evening filled the pub with over 300 adult fans whom had grown up on Mr. Dressup.

Other Programs

Any look at retro decades needs a look at Canadian television over the last 50 years. Speciality networks rerun Canadian classics that many Canadians grew up with. Remember Danger Bay, The Odyssey, Polka Dot Door, Today's Special, The Racoons, Fraggle Rock (yes this Jim Henson Muppet classic was made in Canada), The Forest Rangers, Adventures in Rainbow Country, King of Kensington, Seeing Things, Street Legal, Smith and Smith, Fred Penner's Place, The Elephant Show and the Romper Room, just to name a few Canadian classics?

Sitting in CBC's Museum are a few icons of Canadian television, a trunk and a few puppets. These simple items entertained and delighted several generations of children in English Canada.

There are many unique shows that were produced in Canada over the past fifty years. Here are just a few not mentioned above that were aimed mostly at viewers under 20.

Rice releases another dark thriller

Best-selling author creates another mystery masterpiece

by mike barker
arts&culture

Christopher rice, a 26-year-old american author who has already penned two New York Times bestsellers, has hit the road to promote his newest book, *Light Before Day*.

As with Rice's two previous books, *Density of Soul* and *The Snow Garden*, *Light Before Day* is a dark thriller that revolves around a group of characters who are intertwined in a complex tale of murder, lies and sex. The compelling action and interesting characters makes for a book that is hard to put down.

The story is told through the voice of the main character, Adam Murphy, a man wrestling with personal demons as he follows a trail of murder and disappearances laid out for him like breadcrumbs.

Adam, a 26-year-old journalist and alcoholic who is new to West Hollywood, finds himself on the case of a career-breaking news story he soon discovers he is a part of. While Adam struggles with his own demons—drinking binges that lead to blackouts, coming to terms with the accidental death of his alcoholic mother—he becomes entangled in the disappearances. He also finds himself in the dark world of crystal meth users in West Hollywood's gay community and trailer parks in California's central valley.

For Rice, writing in the first person was a challenge, especially as the character he created had so much to say. "Well if you really get into a single character, he will talk and talk. . . . The second draft was 940 pages long." Through revisions, Rice was able to tell his story more succinctly. The published book is 322 pages and the main character's voice is present but not overwhelming. The other characters are compelling, but we don't know what truly goes on in their minds. The secondary characters each have their time in the story line as the book progresses, but it's Adam that drives the narrative forward.

Rice is a refreshing author who speaks honestly with intelligence and wit. He sees himself as a humble crime writer—which he is proud of—and is hesitant to place himself alongside neither the great Los Angeles crime writers nor notable gay authors. Still, there's no denying that his books are well-researched, well-written page-turners.

Rice leads a new generation of gay writers who speak with a different voice than the previous generation, like Tennessee Williams and Edmond White. His characters are not trying to prove their worth and their sexuality does not dominate the story.

Coming from a family of writers, Rice was encouraged to begin writing as a child. And his parents were always ready to give advice, especially on tackling writer's block.

Bold and artsy: some white space can be good for Helvetica and any design—leaving open space to attract the eye. Run a thumbnail of the book cover being reviewed, creating a visual icon then over emphasizing a common image. The bold headline type is balanced against the light subhead.

NEWS

Faculty returned from the three-week long strike Monday, led by a bagpiper. A moment of silence was observed for fellow instructor John Stammers, who passed away Saturday.
Mike Barker photo

Students and faculty resume semester
Concerns raised after three weeks of missed classes

BY MIKE BARKER
SENIOR REPORTER

COLLEGE FACULTY PARADED BACK TO work ending the three-week strike. Led by a bagpiper the faculty returned to St. James the day before classes resumed.

After last minute negotiations on Friday, March 24, instructors for 24 Ontario colleges agreed to return to the classroom. George Brown College was one of many colleges that decided to resume classes on Tuesday, March 28, while others colleges returned to class the day before.

"We wanted to give [faculty] a day," said Michael Cooke, vice president of academics. "Ideally we would have liked to have given them two or three days, but we felt that that would further penalize the students. At least give the faculty a day to think this through so that when they meet with the students they had a thought through plan."

Faculty returned to classrooms Tuesday to finish the four remaining weeks left this semester. A few programs will continue past the end of the regular semester—Dental Hygiene and Fitness for example—however, most programs will end classes on April 21.

"There are some courses, Dental Hygiene and Fitness, that will actually keep going after April 21, because the students won't have met the outcomes by April 21," said Cooke.

As for the majority of programs faculty have been given room to ensure no student is left behind. One way to give students more time to finish this semester will come from the extension for submitting final marks. Instructors have ten extra days to before marks are due.

"It's also possible within an individual program that if a student needs some more time or some more help just on a personal basis. We try to accommodate that, because our goal is to help each student meet the outcomes," added Cooke.

Class time lost is one concern being raised by students. "I have missed three weeks of classes," said Arlette D'Souza, an international student. "I feel I am completing the semester without the complete course."

For most students, classroom time lost during the strike will not be recouped; instead course material will be condensed. When faculty returned to work, instructors met in consultation with their program chairs to adjust teaching activities to the shorter period.

"The big thing for students is to focus on the outcomes. What are the skills or knowledge that they need at this point in their program," said Cooke.

Cooke further explained "the time and the classes are a means to an end; they're not an end in themselves. Lots of circumstances arise, you're sick, you sleep in, or you have to work. That's not the same as missing the outcomes."

The outcomes can be found in all course outlines handed out at the beginning of each semester by instructors. These learning goals are based on a wider understanding of the course, rather then specific knowledge.

Due to the three weeks without class, students have been asking about a refunds. On March 31, the Ministry for Training, Colleges and Universities released its' decision regarding a refund.

According to Cooke, "The Ministry is saying that any student, who wishes to withdraw because they feel that their success was compromised by the strike, may do so and get a full refund. He further added, "Students hoping for a partial refund will be disappointed with the Ministry's policy."

For a frustrated D'Souza, tuition is not cheap. "I'm a little bit ticked off about the strike because first off, I'm international, I tend to pay around eleven thousand per year and I have to extend my visa if I were to drop this semester and take it again."

"I think there should be a partial refund. In three weeks I've lost a lot of money," added D'Souza. In fact, one week for an international student costs about $367 whereas a domestic student would pay around $80 per week.

When asked about taking some of her concerns to her instructors, D'Souza said, "I think the professors have been pretty concerned about it."

"I took my own concerns to one of my professors and I said if I fail this course I cannot graduate and I don't get to search for a job. And my professor said, 'I've received your projects; I'm going to grade you on them. Don't worry about it.'"

> "I've lost a lot of money," D'Souza

Return to classes marked by tragedy
Faculty march to remember fallen colleage

BY GEORGE BROWN
EDUCTION BEAT

A MOMENT OF SILENCE WAS OBSERVED Monday by returning faculty in honour of John Stammers, a Centennial instructor who passed away over the weekend from the result of an altercation with a car attempting to cross the picket line.

Toronto Police have already decided not to lay criminal charges on the driver, suggesting that the video survilence shows Stammers picking a fight with the car. Police hold Stammers responsible for his own actions and refuse to deal with the matter further, inferred a Police spokesperson last week.

"It's a tragedy and my heart goes out to the family of John [Stammers]. He was only a few years from retirement," said George Adelaide, an instructor at the St. James campus. "I think it's rediculous that the police have suggested John picked the fight with the car. You don't pick a fight with a car—it'll win any day."

While instructors returned to St. James, a bagpiper led a moment of silence and a presession through the three campus building. Students, college staff and security looked on in confusion as the bagpiper mounted through the halls, passed the lone Tim Horton's.

Due to the three weeks without class, students have been asking about a refunds. On March 31, the Ministry for Training, Colleges and Universities released its' decision regarding a refund.

"It's a tragedy and my heart goes out to the family of John [Stammers]. He was only a few years from retirement," said George Adelaide, an instructor at the St. James campus. "I think it's rediculous that the police have suggested John picked the fight with the car. You don't pick a fight with a car—it'll win any day."

While instructors returned to St. James, a bagpiper led a moment of silence and a presession through the three campus building. Students, college staff and security looked on in confusion as the bagpiper mounted through the halls, even through business and finance.

The parade ended on King Street outside the main lobby with a short speech. The faculty then quickly dispereced to their respective departements to begin recovering what was left of the shortened semester through the College's semester completion strategy. The strategy was developed provincewide and for each college. George Brown faculty were then informed of the strategy Monday and given the day to rewrite their courses, dropping some material, but keeping to the expected learning outcomes as set out in each course's syllabus at the beginning of each semester.

PAGE 12
Saturday, December 23, 2006 | THE STUDENT PRESS

Radical and innovative: some presses can allow bleeds along the top or bottom and that feature can be used to run photos off the page, as well as being creative with the navigation. Here the folio/navigation is running in the first column, with another column of white space to separate the two elements.

Childhood memories from the CBC Museum at the CBC Broadcast centre, Tickle-trunk (far left) to Friendly's castle (left)

ARTS

Twelve channels on the dial was enough
Retro Canadian television and the one channel universe

IMAGINE TURNING ON YOUR TELEVISION today to find that you only have one channel to watch and for some reason, it's in black and white. Not so long ago Canadian viewers had very few channels to watch—three in most cities—and cable was not yet popular, as it offered no better choice.

The first Canadian television broadcast began with a news item hosted by Lorne Green—before he left Canada to star in the American western drama Bonanza. Television in Canada started in 1952 with one network broadcasting in English and French, the Canadian Broadcasting Corporation (CBC)/ Société Radio-Canada (SRC). Only Canadians in Toronto and Montreal could watch CBC the first year, but by 1955 the CBC/Radio-Canada had expanded to reach 66 per cent of the Canadian population.

The CBC/Radio-Canada enjoyed nine years dominating the Canadian airwaves, although there had always been American broadcast signals sneaking across the border. In 1961, the CTV Network began broadcasting, with the permission of the CBC—which meant they created their own competition. The CBC controlled broadcasting in Canada until the CRTC was established in 1968.

In the early days of the CRTC, the rules governing Canadian television were established, granting licenses and controlling amounts of Canadian content. 1970 brought the first content regulations making sure that all TV broadcasters in Canada had to fill their schedules with at least 60 per cent Canadian content.

Television grew slightly in the 1970s with the first private French-language network, TVA in 1971 and Global in 1974—as well as educational channels TV Ontario, Access Alberta and B.C.'s Knowledge network. In 1972, Toronto saw the launch of City-TV, which has served as the base for many more channels.

Moses Znaimer, considered a guru of Canadian television, started at the CBC as an interviewer for the program Take 30 (with former Governor General Adrianne Clarkson). Moses helped give birth to City and it's many offspring. When City started broadcasting, it was from the former Electric Circus Nightclub on Queen East.

The explosion on cable did not begin until the mid-1980s when the CRTC allowed pay-TV and speciality channels to open. Canadians finally had more choice as CBC Newsworld, YTV, Vision TV, Muchmusic, pay TV channel Family Channel and many more were all broadcasting by 1987. Since the 80s Canadian cable had grown into the hundreds of channels.

THE PROGRAMS
Any look at retro decades needs a look at Canadian television over the last 50 years. Speciality networks rerun Canadian classics that many Canadians grew up with. Remember Danger Bay, The Odyssey, Polka Dot Door, Today's Special, The Racoons, Fraggle Rock (yes this Jim Henson Muppet classic was made in Canada), The Forest Rangers, Adventures in Rainbow Country, King of Kensington, Seeing Things, Street Legal, Smith and Smith, Fred Penner's Place, The Elephant Show and the Romper Room, just to name a few Canadian classics?

The CBC has embraced their television history with a "retro line" of t-shirts with past CBC logos—from the early days of colour to the evolving familiar logo of today. Currently, a number of items from CBC's children's programming are on display at the CBC Museum at the CBC Broadcast Centre in Toronto. Mr. Dressup's Tickle-trunk and drawing easel and the set from The Friendly Giant can be seen there.

Sitting in CBC's Museum are a few icons of Canadian television, a trunk and a few puppets. These simple items entertained and delighted several generations of children in English Canada.

There are many unique shows that were produced in Canada over the past fifty years. Here are just a few not mentioned above that were aimed mostly at viewers under 20.

THE FRIENDLY GIANT
Over 3000 15-minute episodes were produced between 1958 and 1985 featuring the massive Friendly Giant, played by Bob Homme. Friendly would welcome children at the beginning of each show and then let them into his castle through the drawbridge. Once inside, you were invited to "look up, look w-a-a-a-y up" as the camera panned up to Friendly standing by a window with Jerome the Giraffe and Rusty the Rooster. For over 30 years, Friendly's patient smile welcomed children to enjoy stories, music and humour each weekday morning on CBC.

MR. DRESSUP
Before we had the Tickle-trunk, there was Butternut Square, a show that after 3 years on air led to Mr. Dressup in 1967. Until 1996, the show aired weekday mornings from Toronto with the familiar Mr. Dressup (Ernie Coombs), and two puppets from Butternut Square: Casey, a 4-year old boy and Finnegan (both of whom left in 1990 with their puppeteer Judith Lawrence).

Coombs came to Canada with his friend Fred Rogers—you know, Mr. Rogers—and stayed when Rogers returned to his new American show, Mr. Rogers Neighbourhood. Before leaving, Rogers took a few ideas with him, including the trolley, developed by CBC.

Each day Mr. Dressup would open his Tickle-trunk and pull out a new costume, which he would don for viewers. In 2001, Coombs visited Simon Fraser University in Vancouver to give a "performance" in the campus pub—a chance to record Coombs live with an adult audience for the CBC program Life and Times. That evening filled the pub with over 300 adult fans whom had grown up on Mr. Dressup.

BY MIKE BARKER
CULTURE EDITOR

"Mr. Dressup always took his time. He was patient, wise, and principled..."

Rice releases another dark thriller
Best-selling author creates another mystery masterpiece

CHRISTOPHER RICE, A 26-YEAR-OLD AMERICAN author who has already penned two New York Times bestsellers, has hit the road to promote his newest book, Light Before Day.

As with Rice's two previous books, Density of Soul and The Snow Garden, Light Before Day is a dark thriller that revolves around a group of characters who are intertwined in a complex tale of murder, lies and sex. The compelling action and interesting characters makes for a book that is hard to put down.

The story is told through the voice of the main character, Adam Murphy, a man wrestling with personal demons as he follows a trail of murder and disappearances laid out for him like breadcrumbs.

Adam, a 26-year-old journalist and alcoholic who is new to West Hollywood, finds himself on the case of a career-breaking news story he soon discovers he is a part of. While Adam struggles with his own demons —drinking binges that lead to blackouts, coming to terms with the accidental death of his alcoholic mother—he becomes entangled in the disappearances. He also finds himself in the dark world of crystal meth users in West Hollywood's gay community and trailer parks in California's central valley.

For Rice, writing in the first person was a challenge, especially as the character he created had so much to say. "Well if you really get into a single character, he will talk and talk and talk. . . . The second draft was 940 pages long."

Through revisions, Rice was able to tell his story more succinctly. The published book is 322 pages and the main character's voice is present but not overwhelming. The other characters are compelling, but we don't know what truly goes on in their minds. The secondary characters each have their time in the story line as the book progresses, but it's Adam that drives the narrative forward.

Rice is a refreshing author who speaks honestly with intelligence and wit. He sees himself as a humble crime writer—which he is proud of—and is hesitant to place himself alongside neither the great Los Angeles crime writers nor notable gay authors. Still, there's no denying that his books are well-researched, well-written page-turners.

Rice leads a new generation of gay writers who speak with a different voice than the previous generation, like Tennessee Williams and Edmond White. His characters are not trying to prove their worth and their sexuality does not dominate the story.

Coming from a family of writers, Rice was encouraged to begin writing as a child. And his parents were always ready to give advice, especially on tackling writer's block or finding inspiration.

"One piece of advice that my mother has given me, that I never argued with her on, is write the book that you want to read," he says to the assembled readers in Toronto.

BY MICHEL LEROUX
BOOK EDITOR

Saturday, December 23, 2006 | THE STUDENT PRESS
PAGE 12

Bold and artsy: covers don't have to be complicated, simple can be noticed quickly. This cover offers one simple image—the concept that fits the message of the main story and offers the reader a snapshot that should be recognizable in seconds.

DESIGN · REQUIRES ASSEMBLY

Sophisticated cover: the nameplate need not be complicated and should be allowed breathing room. This cover begins with a news package on the front page. Readers don't like to follow jumps, therefore it's better to run a complete story, even shortened.

STEP THREE
PRODUCTION

PRODUCTION · REQUIRES ASSEMBLY

3.0 Introduction

There are two skills good designers have—design sense and production skills. Without good production skills, the designer has to rely on the pre-press house or printer. A basic knowledge of production goes a long way to understanding what the printer said or avoiding mistakes in print. Of course not everyone is a designer and especially at student newspapers where editors can often be performing layout. The technical aspects of production may seem less foreign than design, yet a rough working knowledge of the other will improve your work.

This book will only scratch the surface of production and while the information is focused on newspaper production, most aspects apply to other areas of design. Check out the handy *Pocket Pal: Graphic Arts Production Handbook* from International Paper—updated every few years, this useful resource covers more topics then you'll need to know. And of course, talk to your printer and learn what you can from them. The production designer/manager/editor/department should have a few other tools aside from a copy of *Pocket Pal*. A loupe is invaluable for examining the fine detail in the final printed page. And a Pantone swatch book for proper color matching is essential.

Production begins with the workflow that is set out for any printed / produced item. A schedule is created and the details help work move smoothly. The small details such as file management, templates and preparation prevent problems at deadline. A paper's production staff usually has a lot of tasks to juggle and there is a good deal of responsibilities including making printing decisions that cost or save money. Saving money one week can mean spending more for better paper on a special issue the next week. Production focuses on the technical aspects of publishing a newspaper. The information covered here is gear specifically to newspaper production—a narrow focus that leaves some knowledge aside. For additional information, there are many other useful resources that cover printing, pre-press and software training.

InDesign Swatches palette: from the Swatches palette pop-up menu, a new blend of CMYK or a Pantone Spot can be added to the list.

Quark Colors: adding CMYK blends and spot colors is also easy in Quark.

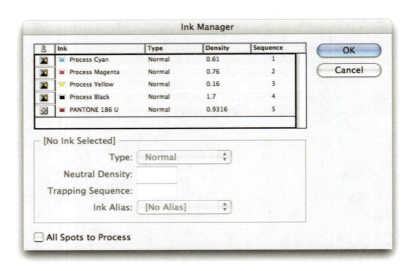

InDesign Ink Manager: InDesign will show you the inks being used in a document, normally CMYK plus spot colors. While ads containing a Pantone spot must keep their set spot color, if the document will be printed in CMYK, all spot colors need to be converted to process. InDesign makes it easy with one button.

PRODUCTION · REQUIRES ASSEMBLY

3.1 Pre-Press

3.1.1 SETTING UP COLOR

Color happens, thanks mostly to advertising or a big printing budget. Plenty of warnings were issued in the Design section (see 2.5.5), but they are worth repeating. Having spot color does not necessarily mean going wild—use spot color sparingly, in a few spots. Full-color is wonderful, save it for photos and graphics, but if color is used on text or graphic elements, treat it as you would a spot color and be aware of your printer's reproduction quality.

Warnings aside, here are a few helpful hints for setting up color in your layout files. As well, keep an eye on color in advertising PDFs. There are a few important things to be aware of, particularly with spot color ads.

INDESIGN:

Adding color in Adobe InDesign is easy. With the **Swatches** palette open, select **New Color Swatch** from the pop-up menu (see below). This will open a window for creating a CMYK blend or choosing a pre-set Pantone color. Select the **Color Type** menu to choose **Spot**, then in the **Color Mode** menu, select **Pantone solid uncoated** to bring up the list of Pantone colors.

When a PDF with a spot color plate is placed in InDesign, the spot color will be added to the Swatches available. This enables that spot color on the page the ad has been placed on, though you will want to save the spot on that page for the ad (does this sentence make sense?). Instead, follow the step above to add the spot color to pages on the same form (see Imposition 3.1.1). The second option on the **Swatches** palette menu is **New Tint Swatch**, which will allow you to set a swatch for a tint of the color swatch you have selected.

QUARK:

To add a color swatch in QuarkXpress, open the **Colors palette** (**F12**) and **right-click** (or ctrl-click) to get the pop-up menu (see below). **Choose New...**, which brings up the **Edit Color** window. If the Colors palette is grayed out, select an object on the pasteboard or from the **Edit** menu, select **Colors...**, which will bring up the Colors window. Click the **New...** button to add a color. Under the **Model** pop-up menu, you can choose either CMYK for a process color or select Pantone solid uncoated. Now you can select the Pantone color, or adjust the CMYK sliders to achieve the color you need.

HOW TO CONVERT SPOT COLOR TO PROCESS IN INDESIGN:

If you have received an image with a spot color in it, such as an ad, the spot color can be stripped from the file, however, InDesign will allow you to convert spot colors used in a layout to Process colors (CMYK). There is further discussion on dealing with spot colors in ads below (see 3.1.4), however, be careful converting an ad's spot color to process. Non-ad images that contain spot colors, such as logos, don't need to run as-is on CMYK pages. Choosing **Ink Manager** from the **Swatches** palette pop-up menu will open a window showing all the color plates in that document. Checking the **All Spots to Process checkbox** will convert the spots in the document so that only the cyan, magenta, yellow and black plates go to press.

3.1.2 IMPOSITION

For a newspaper to be printed, folded and cut in the right order, the individual pages must be assembled to achieve the proper sequence. Referred to as imposition, the process arranges the pages in a somewhat scattered order to have them printed correctly. Page two is always on the reverse of page one, yet if you took your newspaper apart you would find something other than page three next to page two. Not confusing at all, right?

    Chances are you have already noticed this, so the question is, how can this help me? Well if you print a 16-page tabloid paper, knowing that pages 1, 8, 9 and 16 are on the same side of the form, it means those pages get the same color (or colors). The form is the term for your pages assembled together on one printing plane—based on the press size. The finished sheet of page cut to size is your signature. Your printer should be able to supply you with imposition charts to guide your color placement. Every form (in this case a group of four pages) may not be able to receive the same amount of colors—full color may be available on form A and B but only spot color on C, and forget anything other than black

16 PAGE TABLOID

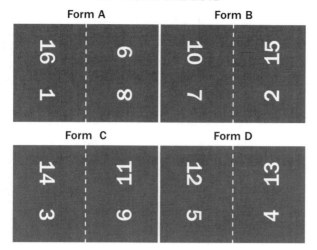

24 PAGE TABLOID

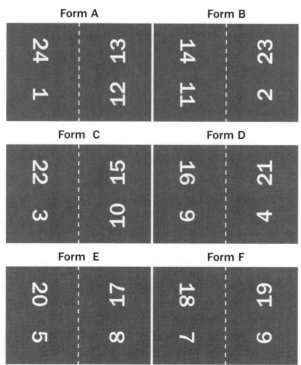

REQUIRES ASSEMBLY · PRODUCTION

on D. There are also limits to the number of pages your printer can print in one pass. Newer web presses—likely at your local daily paper—will be able to handle color on all pages at a cost.

There are ways to add color affordably. Selling a full-color ad for the back will add color to the remaining four pages on that form—the cover and center spread. Maximize the use of color by knowing where to place ads. Spread the color ads around to put full-color on all forms. The same holds true for spot color ads.

Knowing the imposition can also help with designing across two pages side-by-side. Because a paper has a set sequence, designs usually follow from one page to the next, but an image could bleed over the centre gutter from page 6 to 11 if the image relates. Then again, color placement helps the production set up more. Papers trying to make ends meet can group color ads on different pages on the same form and save money on the amount of color printed—also saving money without sacrificing ad placement.

3.1.3   LINES AND DOTS

Printing on newsprint is similar to toilet paper and the quality one can expect is low. Most newspapers are around for a day or just a few, so while quality is an issue, this is balanced with costs. Newsprint is cheap and the down side is the quality of image reproduction. Although this has improved, the paper dictates the line screen. Line screen refers to the number of lines per inch—basically the resolution of the images and text. Most newspapers today get a line screen of 85 lines per inch (lpi) on regular newsprint and 100 lpi on premium—and often coated—stock. Magazines have a starting line screen at 133 lpi up to 175 lpi for high quality art magazines. The small gap between news and magazines illustrates how close the two mediums are. However, uncoated newsprint will soak up ink—although hands covered in newsprint ink makes you wonder—and spread it further, making it hard to get good detail on newsprint.

While you will send your printer a PDF with a higher resolution, it's good practice to save images for your paper's line screen. When scanning or saving a final photograph or bitmapped graphic at size, use double your line screen as your image's resolution (dots per inch or dpi) — in most cases this is 170 dpi for printing at 85 lpi. This is done mostly out of good practice, although leaving your images at 200 or 300 dpi will suffice. However, avoid printing below 170 dpi. A lot of digital images are 72 dpi, but they are quite large, which means they can be shrunk in size and gain more pixels per inch. Web images are 72 dpi and need to be large to print properly without pixilation. When printing images from the web, be aware of this, unless the intentional design is to have a pixilated image.

QuarkXpress users can preview the resolution of an image when importing. Select the image in the Get Picture window and the files details will be listed, including size, color mode and resolution. "Use OPI" might also be selected. Unselect this option now as later it might cause issues with the PDFs you make. It is worth know about OPI, see its own section, 3.5.4 OPI.

3.1.4 ADVERTISING

All newspapers rely on advertising to some degree. Student papers can always some local and national ads to help pay staff and improve the paper. Since advertising brings money into the paper, the ads need to be handled properly.

As PDFs become more widespread and the majority of designers can produce a high-res PDF of an ad, quality has improved. The PDF has a few hidden details you might not be aware of, such as color plates. All ads should be inspected when they are received. Optimally, the PDF should be preflighted with Flightcheck or at the very least Acrobat Professional. Assuming you don't have Flightcheck, open the PDF in Acrobat and select **Preflight...** from the **Document** menu. A window will pop-up with a list a four buttons. Clicking the **PDF/X...** button will open the Preflight: PDF/X window, such as the **Verify...** tool that checks the files compliance with the X-1a standard. Clicking the **Verify...** button brings up a dialog with the option to run extra checks if selected. From this prompt, running the check takes only a few seconds. A dialog with a large green or red dot will appear, whether it checks out or not. If the file did not check out, there is an option in the original Preflight: PDF/X window to save an X-1a version of the file.

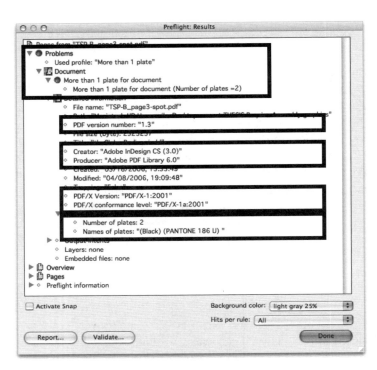

Preflight in Acrobat: some important information can be gained from preflighting a PDF, such as verifying X-1a compliancy, number of plates or layout application used.

Instead of opening the Preflight: PDF/X window, you can choose any of the **Profiles** from the list below Preflight: Profiles. These Profiles will run certain checks, such as checking the file for the number of plates and giving an error result if there are "More than 2 plates". In a full-color document, this would bring up an error, however running the "More than 4 plates" will make sure there are no spot color plates lurking in the PDF.

For example, if an advertiser sent you a PDF ad—that has a photo, ad copy and their logo—which is supposed to be full-color. You run the "More than 4 plates" Profile to find that there are five plates. In the Preflight: Results window, you will see the results, including any errors to the Profile, likely with a red dot next to the headline "Problems". Opening the arrows for Document and then Detailed Information will bring up some hidden secrets in the file, such as the application it originated from, the type of PDF and the distiller or Producer that created the PDF. The PDF/X Version should be "PDF/X-1a:2001", which is the correct compliant version of X-1a.

Below this is another arrow, listing the number of plates and their names. For the file used to create this example image, two plates were found, Black and Pantone 186 U, which means there is an object on that page using the spot color. When checking full-color ads, such an error will mean sending the ad back to the advertiser or agency. Pantone spot colors are used specifically to reproduce a color object exactly—usually a logo or corporate color. Receiving an ad that is black plus one spot does not mean it's meant to be a full-color ad, and the PDF should not be run as process. The Preflight function in Acrobat will allow you to set your own Profile set by choosing the rules and conditions that apply to your workflow, although the list in Acrobat is already extensive.

Often ads are placed in the InDesign file with no errors until exporting that particular page to PDF, such as an OPI error. See 3.5.4 OPI for an explanation on the OPI error.

3.1.5 FONTS

There are a number of font file formats that have evolved over the years. The first digital fonts were bitmap typefaces, which displayed a pixelized representation of each letter—now gone from modern computers, bitmapped fonts can still be seen on cellphones. PostScript fonts came along to offer scaleable type, a draw back of bitmap fonts. PostScript typefaces render letterforms using the PostScript language and there is are separate file formats for Mac and PC. TrueType is a format common for both Mac and PC, although InDesign may not correctly output the TrueType to a PDF. TrueType was popular for free or novelty fonts and if such fonts are necessary for a design, outline the text set in TrueType before creating the PDF.

The newest font format is OpenType, which was developed to replace PostScript and TrueType, with one format for by Mac and PC. OpenType fonts can contain as many as 65,000 glyphs (or characters)—TrueType and PostScript can only handle 256 glyphs—and OpenType can have more advanced typographic features.

3.2 Production Management

Managing the production workflow is an important part of a successful newspaper. Done right, production can be done affordably, efficiently and timely. Production on an issue can go smoothly with the right planning ahead of time. This section offers just a few ways of organizing production.

3.2.1 SCHEDULE/WORK-BACK

One thing you can rarely change is the deadline set by your printer. Your readers want the paper on the day they always expect to see it. A weekly or bi-weekly paper should set a firm printing deadline with their printer—likely the printer will insist upon it. A monthly paper may have a few days to wiggle with, unless your paper is always available the first Monday of every month. With your printing schedule, create a production schedule. This will be based on how many workers will be doing layout and how many pages in each issue. Some papers rely on all section editors to lay out their section, while other papers have a few dedicated production workers. Either way, most are students who have to work around those pesky classes.

All PDFs are needed at 10pm Tuesday night in order to be printed overnight and delivered at 8am. Now work backward. There is time needed for uploading the PDFs to the printer's FTP, time to distill the PDFs, time for finally edits, first edits and layout. Decide on the workflow your paper will use to lay out and proof pages. Allow time for proofing the final PDFs. All told, you may need ten hours or 23 hours to get the paper laid out. You may also be able to stagger the due time for each section so that features and arts are due to the production department Sunday at 5pm, news and sports are due at 5pm on Monday. Set the deadlines with your editors and help them meet the expectations.

The reality with deadlines is that most people feel they can squeeze extra time. Even with three production workers laying out three arts pages, not all copy is needed immediately at 5pm, but the majority is due. The professional way to handle any deadline is keeping all parties informed. Letting someone know the deadline will be missed by a few hours is far more professional then being several hours late without any communication. Once you have written the schedule, post the key milestones on the office wall for all to see. During your editorial planning meetings, ensure appropriate deadlines are set. But, be prepared for change.

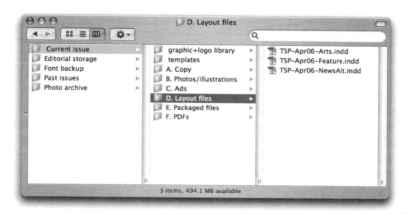

File management: keeping production files organized kelps keep the production workflow moving. The simplest system would be to keep one issues files together and organize past issues into an archive.

3.2.2 FILE MANAGEMENT

Managing the computer files used to publish each issue can be a simple task and help keep your newsroom organized. Depending on the number of computers in your newsroom, you may have one dedicated computer or a server to handle file storage. Network hard drives are fairly cheap for three or four computers or a proper file server—any computer with a big hard drive and left alone in the corner—to allow more users access.

Find an organizing strategy that works for your paper—or make sure your paper is following one that's in place. Have a current issue folder only for the in-production issue and archive all past issues. In the current issue folder devise a scheme for sorting the elements of your paper, numbered or lettered for the workflow: A. Copy; B. Photos/illustrations; C. Ads; D. Layout files; E. Packaged files; F. PDFs

You might also leave a folder in there permanently for your repeating elements: staff photos, paper and association logos and templates. Staying organized will prevent files from wandering onto the desktop then into the trash. Even still, label the files with the paper's name and issue number.

Backing up files is always recommended, but time allowing, grab copies of images from each issue and put them into a photo archive folder, which can save another editor from searching for the photo of your school's President or an often-in-the-news Dean, professor, coach or national student government hack.

3.2.3 GOING TO PRINT

Newsrooms are busy and chaotic around the final hours of deadline but there are many things to consider—taken in a calm moment. Below is a production checklist of sample things to check before sending your paper to the press. Write one that fits for your paper. Mistakes are made in the final hours of production, yet most can be avoided.

As the production or design staff you will be concerned with the look and visual quality of the paper, but you should still consider yourself a journalist—read your paper, report typos and spelling mistakes to the copy editor or fix them. The copy editor and other editors may notice a design element you missed.

Adobe InDesign and QuarkXpress both have an excellent feature worth trying. When the layout file is complete, in InDesign, choose **Package** from the **File** menu or in QuarkXpress, choose **Collect for Output** on the **File** menu. Better yet, if you use InDesign, choose the option above, **Preflight**. This will run a check on the file and its linked files prior to packaging the files. After InDesign has analyzed the files (which will take less than a minute), a window will pop-up with any warnings concerning issues with the fonts or linked files—such as which images are RGB. If everything checked out, the **Package** button can be pressed to package the file.

Packaging/Collecting for output will save a copy of your layout file, fonts and images into a separate folder. Close the original file and open the copy, which should have the images linked. Do this to make sure all images and ads are properly linked to your

InDesign: Package

Quark: Collect for Output

InDesign & Quark: both applications have an option that copies images, fonts and layout file to a separate folder. Indesign (left) also has a Preflight option as well.

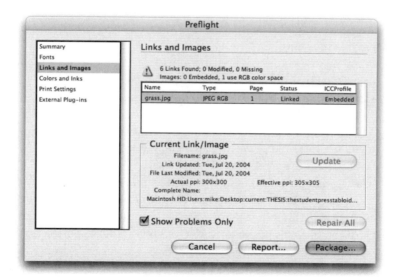

InDesign Preflight window: errors will be flagged before packaging the files, helping catch mistakes. In the window above, InDesign found that one of the files is an RGB JPEG.

file—notice that you will be warned during the Packaging/Collecting process that files are missing. The newsroom is a busy place and sometimes production staff and editors become a little less organized. Linking an important full-color full-page ad from one computer's desktop and then ripping the PDF on another may break the link—and a bitmapped low resolution ad runs for which you can't issue an invoice.

For best results, create your PDFs or do your final print from the packaged file, knowing that the packaged file will have all the images and ads linked correctly.

Finally, check the PDF section below for more PDF workflow suggestions, however, always look at your final PDF—even print and proof—for any last minute errors. The packaged file is also useful for archiving. Archiving the packaged folders and PDFs into an archive folder will save time as the files are already organized and nothing should be missing. The PDF serves as a digital photocopy of each issue—a document that should be able to be opened in the distant future.

3.2.4 FINAL PRODUCTION CHECKLIST

- All ads received
- Viewed or Flightchecked all ad PDFs.
- Packaged or Collected for Output each layout file.
- Outputted final PDFs in X-1a format from the Packaged files (InDesign) or outputted EPS/PS files from Quark files, then Distilled EPS into X-1a PDFs
- Viewed all final PDFs and checked the following:
  - All ads are in place
  - Zoomed close up to ads to double check quality
  - Printed PDFs as necessary to read through and inspect final files before sending to printer
- Account for all pages uploaded to the FTP server.

3.5 PDF 101

PDF or Portable Document File is an Adobe invention that combines their Postscript and EPS technology into a file that is meant to be universally viewable as WYSIWYG (What You See Is What You Get, pronounced wizzy-wig). Postscript is a language Adobe created for computers to talk to laser printers to get the best possible image quality. They can be interactive and have embedded movies. They can also be high-quality print ready for reproduction on a digital printer or full color web press. For your purpose, you will want to create the industry standard PDF/X-1a (see 3.5.1 for an explanation).

Whether your paper uses InDesign or Quark Xpress, have a copy of Adobe Acrobat Professional—this includes the full version of Acrobat and Distiller. Unless you are running InDesign CS1 (3.0) or newer make sure you are creating your PDFs using Distiller. Quark Xpress does not use an Adobe version of the PDF engine and for best results, output a Postscript (PS) file for Distiller. InDesign and Quark can output raw PS files or EPS that can be later processed by Distiller. This is done by printing to a file using a PDF printer. Basically, the Postscript file is created using a postscript printer (or it's description file) to process the data into the Postscript language. PDFs range in quality and size based on their purpose.

3.5.1 THE RIGHT FORMAT

There is a right way and many wrong ways to make a PDF. The right way is probably the best way. This section explains the correct format for sending your newspaper to the printer—PDF/X-1a. X-1a is an industry standard for PDF technology based on Acrobat 4.0 (PDF version 1.3) standards. Basically, all the printers and 3rd-party pre-press equipment manufacturers who used PDF technology were getting concerned with the growing number of PDF versions—two. It didn't help matters that designers could output a PDF with a wide range of settings enabled or not at all, including correctly embedded fonts. This led to the creation of an ISO compliant standard for graphic content exchange. Every company and printer now agrees that a PDF/x-1a: 2001 will always follow the same criteria. PDF technology has been improved since PDF version 1.3 became the version X-1a PDFs would conform to—the current version of the application, Acrobat 7 uses PDF version 1.6, yet X-1a is back in the late nineties.

Just for those confused right now, each version of Adobe's PDF application suite (Acrobat Professional and Acrobat Distiller) has created a numbered version of the PDF standard. New features are compatible with the new version.

The settings in InDesign or Quark for X-1a should not be changed—and in fact any change will make the file not an X-1a. In any case, ask your printer for their preferred format. Below is a description of the process for exporting PDFs in both InDesign and QuarkXpress. However, your printer's pre-press department may suggest a different way, especially for Quark—use their settings and visit the pre-press department to see a demo if necessary.

Other PDF formats include: Web or Screen, at 72 dpi and RGB screen colors, no for print; Print, Press, super-high quality PDF with 1200 dpi resolution, overkill for a newspaper and creates a large file.

3.5.2 INDESIGN

Exporting to PDF is a simple task in InDesign, however, for best results there are two ways to approach exporting PDFs depending on your version of InDesign. CS and CS2 will export a compliant PDF/X-1a. Attempting to change any settings in the Export window will result in the PDF becoming a custom preset. Unfortunately, there is no such format as PDF/X-1a-and-one-little-change—once a change is made, it is no longer an X-1a. That includes adding bleed settings, which don't normally affect newspapers. So, no changes are allowed, except exporting a single-page or spread. Most printers will allow the centre spread to be printed as one image, however, you have to export the spread as one file.

Versions of InDesign before CS do not export PDF/X-1a compliant PDFs. In this case, export an EPS file for each page and distill it through Acrobat Distiller set to PDF/X-1a. An X-1a compliant file will be created.

[Screenshot of Export PDF dialog]

InDesign PDF export: changing options under the PDF/X-1a export will result in a custom export, not X-1a compliant PDF.

3.5.3 QUARK

As mentioned above, Quark does not use the Adobe PDF engine, but a third party engine—for some reason, Adobe didn't want to license it to Quark. This means making a PDF in Quark is less reliable. You cannot simply choose the PDF/X-1a setting to get a compliant PDF. However, the PDF you can produce from Quark is still good for proofing. In order to export a compliant PDF, output either an EPS (export each page as an EPS, then distill) or PS file (print to a PS file then distill that file). An EPS is basically an image file containing type, vector and bitmap images, which is written in Postscript and encapsulated (Encapsulated PostScript). The EPS file is more versatile then a PS file and can still be distilled.

3.5.4 OPI

OPI (Open Pre-press Interface) is not a file format, but a part of the Postscript language that substitutes high-resolution (hires) image files with low-resolution (lores) previews. OPI was developed as part of the EPS format—a file format that includes postscript comments to specify how the file is to be handed by desktop publishing software. Aldus, the inventors of PageMaker, and now a part of Adobe invented OPI when desktop publishing was done on much slower computers. Today the need to replace "hires" with "lores" is unnecessary as modern computers can handle the large image files and display them in high-resolution more easily and modern software, such as InDesign, is able to substitute high-resolution images within the application. Designer can still use OPI when using large image files—for the designer the "lores" image will be used, and then substituted by the pre-press operator's computer. When exporting from InDesign, the graphics can be omitted, but the OPI comments remain embedded in the file for the pre-press software. InDesign can also substitute the "hires" back into the file during export.

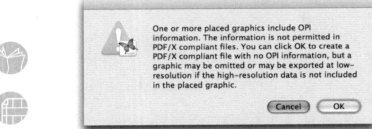

OPI error: when exporting a PDF from InDesign, the above error might occur if one of the placed graphics—either in EPS or PDF format—in the file contains Open Pre-press Interface (OPI) comments used for substituting high resolution images on screen with a low resolution placeholder. For a PDF/X-1a file to meet standards, the PDF cannot contain OPI information, in case the "hires" image were to become separated and thus cause the file to not compliant.

PDF ISSUES AND OPI:

Eventually an OPI issue will come up at your PDF, especially if your newspaper used InDesign, exports pages in PDF format and receive PDF ads. As mentioned above, the best format for exporting a PDF from InDesign is PDF/X-1a, however an X-1a compliant file does not support OPI image substitution. The warning will come when the final page containing an offending PDF or EPS is exported from InDesign. If the original PDF or

EPS was created properly clicking Okay to create an X-1a compliant file should work. After the export, make sure to inspect the page in Acrobat—zoom in and look at the image, if it's heavily pixilated then there is a problem. Most likely the PDF contained both a "hires" and "lores" version of the image and was able to substitute the image correctly.

Another option is to use the "Show import options" feature when placing the original PDF or EPS into the InDesign document. The window will appear with several import options—by default the "Use TIFF or PICT Preview" is selected. Choosing "Rasterize the PostScript" is one option for importing the correct image will, as is selecting "Read Embedded OPI Image Links". The reason for selecting "Read Embedded OPI Image Links" is to ensure the image is embedded at that moment rather then relying on the pre-press operator to do later. PDF files are meant to be completely self-contained without extra files attached, as can be the case with EPS files.

However, if for some reason the "hires" image was never embedded in the original file, this will have no effect. Once the PDF or EPS is placed in InDesign, select the placed file and change its Display Performance to "High Quality Display"—if any of the images embedded in the file disappear, then the PDF or EPS was created without the "hires" image.

QUICK REFERENCE CHART

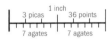

AGATE	PICA	INCH
7	3	0.5
14	6	1.0
21	9	1.5
28	12	2.0
25	15	2.5
42	18	3.0
49	21	3.5
56	24	4.0
63	27	4.5
70	30	5.0
77	33	5.5
84	36	6.0
91	39	6.5
98	42	7.0
105	45	7.5
112	48	8.0
119	51	8.5
126	54	9.0
133	57	9.5
140	60	10.0
147	63	10.5
154	66	11.0
161	69	11.5
167	72	12.0
175	75	12.5
182	78	13.0
189	81	13.5
196	84	14.0
203	87	14.5
210	90	15.0
217	93	15.5
224	96	16.0
231	99	16.5
238	102	17.0

16 PAGE TABLOID

Form A — 16, 6, 1, 8
Form B — 10, 15, 7, 2
Form C — 14, 11, 3, 9
Form D — 12, 13, 5, 4

20 PAGE TABLOID

Form A — 20, 11, 1, 10
Form B — 12, 19, 9, 2
Form C — 18, 13, 3, 8
Form D — 14, 17, 7, 4
Form E — 16, 5
Form F — 15, 6

24 PAGE TABLOID

Form A — 24, 13, 1, 12
Form B — 14, 23, 11, 2
Form C — 22, 15, 3, 10
Form D — 16, 21, 9, 4
Form E — 20, 17, 5, 8
Form F — 18, 19, 7, 6

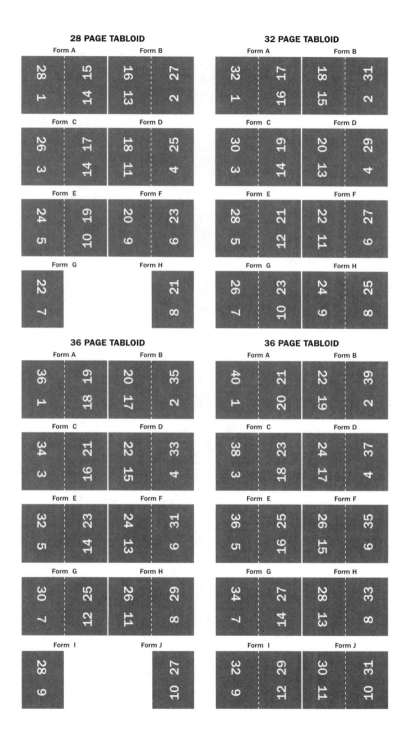

REQUIRES ASSEMBLY · PRODUCTION   **107**

A

advertising *22, 23, 28, 31, 58, 61, 64*
agate *28*
Arnold, Edmund C. *17*
asymmetrical *13*

B

barker *28*
baseline *28, 39*
Berliner *22, 24, 26, 28*
Bild *22*
blackletter *28*
bleed *28*
broadsheet *21, 22, 23, 26, 27, 28, 31, 34, 59*
byline *50*

C

camera-ready *28*
caption *28*
centre spread *28*
Character Styles *65*
cmyk *28*
colour *70*
colour separation *28*
colour swatch *28*
columns *21, 34, 35, 36, 37, 43, 47, 50, 53, 59, 61, 64, 74*
continuous tone *28*
corona *41*
cursive *28*

D

deck *21, 28, 30, 47, 49, 50*
design principles *12*.
   See Principles of Design
dominant element *55*
dot gain *29*

double truck *28*

E

em *29*
en *29*
eps *29*
Excelsior *41*

F

flag *28, 29, 30*
folio *18, 29, 54, 55, 57*
font *29*
form *29*
Frankfurter Allgemeine *22*
Functional News Design *17*

G

Globe and Mail *23, 42*
gothic *29*
grid *vi, 34, 59, 64*
Gutenberg *24, 25, 38*

H

hairline *29*
halftone *29*
headline *12, 18, 21, 28, 29, 30, 46, 47, 48, 49, 50, 51, 55, 59, 74, 75*

I

imposition *29, 70*
InDesign *45, 64, 65*
info-graphic.
   See Information graphics
information boxes *53*
information graphics *75*
Info box.
   See information boxes

K
kerning *29, 48*
kicker *30*

L
La Presse *23*
leading *30, 38, 40, 44, 45*
Le Devoir *42*
legibility *21, 38, 40*
library *68*
Linotype *25*

M
M *30*
masthead *30, 58*
moirÈ *30*
Montreal *23, 37, 42*

N
nameplate *18, 23, 28, 29, 30, 31, 58, 62, 71*
Nested Styles *65*
Nimrod *41*
nutgraph *21*

O
offset *30*
over-banner *30*

P
package *59*
page hierarchy *54*
Pantone *70, 72*
Paragraph styles *65*
pica *30*
pilcrow *37*
Pi Sheng *24*
Postscript *42*

Principles of Design *12*
    Balance *13*
    Contrast *12*
    Emphasis *12*
    Frame of reference *15*
    Gestalt/unity *16*
    Movement/direction *14*
    Positive/negative space *14*
    Repetition *15*
    Unity/gestalt *16*
principles of news design *18*
process colours *28, 31*
pull-quote *21, 31, 51, 52, 53, 55*

Q
Quark *45, 64, 67*

R
readability *17, 18, 34, 35, 37, 38, 43, 44, 59*
register *31*

S
saddle stitch *31*
screen angles *31*
script *31*
sidebars *51*
skybox *24, 31, 62*
Society for News Design *22, 27*
spot colour *31, 70, 71, 73*
spread *61*.
    See also Double-truck
square serif *31*
style-sheets *64*
style guide *68*
subtractive primaries *31*
symmetrical *13*

T

tabloid *vi, 17, 21, 22, 26, 27, 28, 31, 34, 35, 57, 68, 71*
template *iv, 61, 64, 68, 74*
The Guardian *22, 26*
Toronto Star *26, 42*
Typeface
    Bell Gothic *41*
    Corona *41*
    Excelsior *41*
    Frutiger *41*
    Miller *42*
    News Gothic *41*
    Nimrod *41*
    Times Europa *41*
    Torstar *42*
    Trade Gothic *41*
    Utopia *41*
    Walburn *42*

W

web offset *31*
window *21*

X

x-height *39, 41, 43*

Colophon

Book & Typography

Mike Barker, of Toronto and Vancouver, designed and produced this book. The text face for this book is the Lino Letter family (Linotype). Headlines and additional text is set in ITC Franklin Gothic and Barker Gothic.

Mike Barker

Born in Winnipeg, raised in B.C. and currently working in Toronto, Mike has worked for several newspapers and magazines including Adbusters, Medusa Magazine, The Globe and Mail, The Peak Newspaper (Simon Fraser University) and The Dialog Newspaper (George Brown College), as well as having freelanced and redesigned several more. Mike received a BA from Simon Fraser University in History and Communications and attended George Brown College's 3-year graphic design program.

The Author Wishes to Thank

Ron Johnson at Kansas State University for his insights into news design both at the Canadian University Press National Conference (Toronto, 2006) and Associate Colligate Press Spring Conference (Los Angles, 2006); to the Society of News Design and the many news designers around the world who inspire and continuously improve news design; Sean Patrick Sullivan in Toronto for some proofreading assistance; special thanks to Shelley Warsh (and other George Brown Faculty including Diane Erlich and Ian Gregory); to the friends and family (Mom and Dad especially) for the much needed support; to classmates for hearing endlessly about news design for the last four months or several years depending on who one talks to; and finally to Andrea Warner, my brilliant editor.